HEALTHY CONGREGATIONS

HEALTHY CONGREGATIONS

A Systems Approach

Peter L. Steinke

THE
ALBAN
INSTITUTE
Herndon, Virginia
www.alban.org

The Alban Institute
2121 Cooperative Way, Suite 100
Herndon, VA 20171

Unless otherwise indicated, scripture quotations in this volume are from the New Revised Standard Version of the Bible, copyright © 1989 by the Division of Christian Education of the National Council of the Churches of Christ in the United States of America. Used by permission. All rights reserved.

Scripture quotations marked KJV are from The Holy Bible, King James Version.

Scripture quotations marked NEB are from The New English Bible, copyright © The Delegates of the Oxford University Press and The Syndics of the Cambridge University Press, 1961, 1970.

Scripture quotations marked RSV are from the Revised Standard Version of the Bible, copyright © 1946, 1952, 1971, by the Division of Christian Education of the National Council of the Churches of Christ in the U.S.A. Used by permission.

The author also gratefully acknowledges permission to reprint the following:

Excerpt from *Dakota*. Copyright © 1993 by Kathleen Norris. Reprinted by permission of Ticknor & Fields/Houghton Mifflin Co. All rights reserved.

Excerpt from *In Pursuit of the Great White Rabbit*. Reprinted with permission from *In Pursuit of the Great White Rabbit* by Edward Hays, copyright Forest of Peace Publishing, Inc., 251 Muncie Road, Leavenworth, KS 66048-4946.

Excerpt from *The Way of the Sufi* by Idries Shah. Copyright © 1968 by Idries Shah. Used by permission of Dutton Signet, a division of Penguin Books USA Inc.

Cover design by Concept Foundry.

Library of Congress Cataloging-in-Publication Data

Steinke, Peter L.
  Healthy congregations : a systems approach / Peter L. Steinke. -- [2nd ed.].
    p. cm.
  Includes bibliographical references.
  ISBN-13: 978-1-56699-330-2
  ISBN-10: 1-56699-330-X
  1. Church controversies. 2. Parishes--Psychology. 3. System theory. I. Title.

  BV652.9.S73 2006
  250.1'1--dc22

                          2006036118

      10   09   08   07   VG   2   3   4   5

Contents

Foreword   vii

Preface 2006   ix

Preface 1996   xi

PART 1   WHOLENESS

Chapter 1   Life Is All of a Piece   3

Chapter 2   Ten Principles of Health   15

Chapter 3   Promoting Healthy Congregations   25

PART 2   DISEASE PROCESS

Chapter 4   Congregations at Risk   43

Chapter 5   Infectious Anxiety   57

Chapter 6   The Coconut Captivity of the Church   73

PART 3   HEALTH RESOURCES

Chapter 7   The Higher Medicines   85

Chapter 8   The Immune Congregation   95

Chapter 9   An Ounce of Prevention Is Worth a Pound of Intervention   107

Notes   117

Bibliography   123

Foreword

There are few, if any, pastors or counselors in the church who understand and communicate clearly what the Family Systems approach is better than Dr. Peter Steinke.

The author of the conflict resolution process called Bridge-Builders has now provided the preventative prescription for such situations in this writing which enables congregations to be proactive in maintaining a healthy attitude and atmosphere within the relational body they share together. The clarity of presentation, combined with superb illustrations and examples from other disciplines, especially medicine, as well as biblically based connections, allows the reader a way to grasp the essence of what healthy communities look like.

This book should be one of the resources used in church leadership retreats as well as in general adult education classes. Having a sense of how the interaction effects and affects the whole body can provide the necessary checks and balances within the congregational setting as it seeks to move forward in its mission and ministry. A healthy body does not happen by accident and having a prescriptive resource available, like this one, is an invaluable asset to life together and for the sake of the whole mission of the church.

Bishop Paul J. Blom
Texas-Louisiana Gulf Coast Synod (ELCA)

Preface 2006

Soon after I had written *Healthy Congregations,* I was contacted by Lutheran Brotherhood in Minneapolis (now known as Thrivent Financial for Lutherans), a financial service company, concerning a partnership in developing assistance for congregations. I suggested elaborating on my new book and developing a series of workshops for lay leaders with the same name—Healthy Congregations. For nine years they financially supported the project, which led to the training of more than 1500 facilitators in 26 denominations. The Healthy Congregations effort is now located at Trinity Lutheran Seminary in Columbus, Ohio.

The interest in creating and sustaining healthy congregations is obviously widespread. Many leaders in churches have mentioned how helpful it is to have some "standards" or "markers" by which to gauge their congregations' health. They realized, for instance, that as challenge to our physical bodies through exercise is health promoting, so challenge is to the "body of Christ."

If I were to make any changes in the original manuscript today, I would place more emphasis on the key role of "mood, tone, and spirit" in enhancing congregational health, not unlike what we've learned about the relationship between attitude and social connections and our health. There are an increasing number of "depressed" congregations, ones that succumb to helplessness and hopelessness, especially as they continue to decline in membership, face a changing neighborhood, or "stay stuck" in monotonous or distressful patterns. They find it hard to maintain joy and vitality. Their dispirited mood limits their energy and imagination, the very resources they need to revitalize themselves. I wonder if the "mood, tone, and spirit" of a congregation isn't closely related to having a clear purpose, which in healthy congregations is a focus on mission. When life is meaningful, people have more energy—and hope. The philosopher Fredrich Nietzche said that if Christians wanted others to believe in their Redeemer, they needed to look more redeemed.

Preface 1996

This book is about the stewardship of the congregation: how people care for, respond to, and manage their life together. It is about holding in trust the well-being of the congregation. The health of a congregation involves the stewardship of the congregation as a unit in itself. In the introduction to *Healthy People 2000,* Dr. Louis W. Sullivan, former U.S. Secretary of Health and Human Services, declared, "Personal responsibility, which is to say responsible and enlightened behavior by each and every individual, truly is the key to good health."[1] Health is promoted by personal activity. Health comes from measures that each person can affect.

The same could be said for a larger organism, such as a congregation. Like healthy people, congregations promote their health through "responsible and enlightened behavior." The people who are most in position to enhance the health of a congregation are precisely those who have been empowered to be responsible, namely the leaders. They are the chief stewards; they are the people who are willing to be accountable for the welfare of the congregation. They set a tone, invite collaboration, make decisions, map a direction, establish boundaries, encourage self-expression, restrain what threatens the integrity of the whole, and keep the congregation's direction aligned with its purposes.

To address questions about the health of a congregation, we need to have in mind some picture of what health means. Health is wholeness. Health means all the parts are working together to maintain balance. Health means all the parts are interacting to function as a whole. Health is a continuous process, the ongoing interplay of multiple forces and conditions.

Health is not the absence of disease. Health and disease are not opposites. Physician Larry Dossey claims, "The paradox, carved into our biology: life and health depend on illness and cannot exist without it."[2] Disease disrupts the body's balance. By doing so, disease provokes the healing capacities of the body to restore the very balance disease has disrupted. Many of the "symptoms" of disease are actually the body's healing resources at work (for example, higher body temperature kills germs).

To talk about a healthy congregation is to talk about a congregation from an organic perspective. Only organisms can be said to be healthy or diseased. Only living systems are characterized by wellness or illness, soundness or injury, balance or disorder. In fact, the mark of organic life is the continuing play of balance and imbalance. When an organism's balance fails to some degree, or when the organism remains in a state of instability for too long a time, it is sick. When the whole process fails, the organism dies. Thus health is the capacity for life, what an organism must do to persevere. Health is the ability of a living system to respond to a wide assortment of challenges to its integrity.

How appropriate is the organic view for understanding healthy congregations? The New Testament speaks of the church as a living system, akin to the human body. The "body of Christ" as a metaphor for the church appears thirty-seven times. Christ is identified as the "head" of the body in seven references. What the apostle Paul wanted to make clear is that the "body of Christ" is a whole composed of many parts, yet it functions as one. The various members and subsystems of a congregation interweave, much as do the organs of the human body with the ongoing interaction of cells, blood flow, nerve endings, energy sources, and waste products.

It is easy to impose institutional values on health, as reflected in the phrase "healthy, growing churches." An organic view, however, prevents us from imposing on health a meaning it does not have. Organic processes are not linear. They are not merely progressive or expansive. Some organic processes promote growth through decay, shedding, and breakdown. Some organic growth is downward—a deepening, a rooting, a maturing process. An organic view will not allow us to make health synonymous with enlargement and mass. Organic life comes in many sizes and shapes, all of which may be said to be healthy.

At times health is manifested by growth in size. At other times health involves sheer maintenance, with little or no growth at all. The Western idea of growth is "get big, get strong, and win." Westerners assume an increase in size will ensure continuation or survival of the organism. Unfortunately this understanding is carried over into notions about congregational health. Growing churches are assumed to be healthy, especially in contrast to what are called "maintenance" churches. Congregations engaged in upkeep are disparaged, even relegated to the realm of the "diseased." "Maintenance" becomes a pejorative term. After all, work involving housekeeping tasks brings the lowest wages and requires the lowest skills. Yet the word *maintenance* itself is positive. It derives from *main* (hand) and *teneo* (keep). It is caring for something by hand. It is managing. A large part of health is maintenance (brushing teeth, washing hands, taking vitamins, exercising).

We do a great disservice to congregations whose growth is minimal, static, or even in decline when we say they are unhealthy without regard to their stage of development or context. Most of the time whether a church expands is a matter of demographics, totally unrelated to health issues. Organically, nothing grows forever. Growth ceases sooner or later.

Do not construe lack of growth as a sign of health. Healthy entities do grow in size and numbers. The point is that they do not *only* grow. What contributes to the unhealth of a "maintenance congregation" is *low* maintenance—neglect, indifference, helplessness, passivity, entrenched hostilities, rigidity, carelessness, low energy—essentially poor stewardship of the congregation. If these congregations were to become *high* maintenance, they would enjoy carefully and intentionally designed growth in other areas.

In her book *Dakota,* Kathleen Norris describes Hope Presbyterian Church in South Dakota as a high maintenance congregation. She characterizes Hope as "small, dying, and beautifully alive." But it's healthy. During a fifteen-year period, Hope's membership declined from forty-six to twenty-five, yet its donation for mission increased every year. Norris says Hope gives people "a sense of identity," provides a "hospitable place," and remains "so alive to the world."[3] Health is not an end but a means to fulfill the purpose of life. Health is a resource for life, not the object of living. Indeed health is not the meaning of a congregation's existence, but a congregation fulfills its meaning in conditions of health and disease. How, then, can a congregation optimize its health to advance its mission? How can we tell whether a congregation is moving in a healthy direction? What limits healthy congregational functioning? What kinds of responses promote congregational health?

In this book, we will view the congregation as one organism. Any organism, from bacteria through the vast range of plants, insects, animals to human beings, is a living system. In a systems approach, we look beyond the trees and see the forest. We keep the total picture in mind. Instead of seeing separate, unrelated parts, we see interrelated parts. Rather than looking at discrete objects, we see their interactions. A systems perspective offers a more panoramic view of what is happening. Health and illness depend on all the parts interacting; no single part or group promotes health or illness. Everyone contributes. The congregation is seen as the unit of health or illness.

The first part of the book, "Wholeness," provides the conceptual framework and a common ground for discussion of the question, what is health? In chapter 1, "Life Is All of a Piece," various examples demonstrate how parts interact to form a whole. The second chapter, "Ten Principles of Health," lays out what advances the health of an organism and derives from that clues

to the health of an organization. "Promoting Healthy Congregations," the third chapter, presents seven responses that promote
the health principles described in the previous chapter. It speaks
to the question of why some congregations are located toward
the positive end of the health and disease continuum and what
makes them move toward this end, whatever their location on
the continuum at any given time.

Part two, "Disease Process," is not intended to measure a
congregation's "sickness" or "dysfunction." Rather it illustrates
how disease processes are enabled. Health and disease involve
choices and actions. The first chapter in this section, "Congregations at Risk," presents a number of case studies that point to
the potential risks to congregational health. The next chapter,
"Infectious Anxiety," describes specific interactions that disease an organism, and likewise an organization. "The Coconut
Captivity of the Church," chapter 6, sets forth the particular
danger rigidity poses for the health of a congregation.

The third part, "Health Resources," addresses the stewardship of the congregation. "Higher Medicines" is a theological
discussion of healthy congregations. It looks at how beliefs influence behavior, how the "mutual conversation and consolation" of
the members of the body affect health, and how meaningfulness
affects health. The second chapter of this section, "The Immune
Congregation," speaks precisely to the role of leadership in
stimulating health. The head of a body is the primary organ for
healthy bodily functioning. The chief stewards of a congregation play a similar role. Finally, the chapter called "An Ounce
of Prevention Is Worth a Pound of Intervention" offers several
approaches to congregational health promotion. What is at stake
in healthy congregational functioning is not mere survival but
that "we are to grow up in every way into him who is the head,
into Christ," that we are to upbuild our life together in love,
and that we are to give a vital witness to the One St. Matthew
describes: "He took our infirmities and bore our diseases" (Matthew 8:17).

PART 1

WHOLENESS

Chapter 1

Life Is All of a Piece

The whole earth is alive, all of a piece, one living thing, a creature.

—Lewis Thomas

Each of us is an essential atom in a living, breathing, and changing organism.

—Max DePree

No animal or plant is self-sustaining. The quest to be alone is indeed a futile one, never successfully followed in the history of life.

—George Gaylord Simpson

From atom to organism to person, the pattern that meets us in nature is that of connection and contact. In the world of living organisms, isolation is nowhere met.

—Larry Dossey

A Systems Approach

Systems thinking is basically a way of thinking about life as all of a piece. It is a way of thinking about how the whole is arranged, how its parts interact, and how the relationships between the parts produce something new. A systems approach claims that any person or event stands in relationship to something. You cannot isolate anything and understand it. The parts function as they do because of the presence of the other parts. All parts interface and affect each other. Their behaviors are reciprocal

3

to one another, mutually reinforcing. Thus change in one part produces change in another part, even in the whole. There is a "ripple" through the system.

No problem can be seen in isolation. The problem is in the whole, not the part. The system is the locus of the problem. The problem is in the interaction between the parts. The same is true for solutions and corrections.

System thinking is basic to understanding life processes. "When we are working with living systems," psychologist Edgar Jackson says, "we are dealing with process, not substance."[1] In a systems approach, we look at the health of a congregation as a process. Health is not a state or a thing. Health is a manifestation of processes, many hidden yet real.

A SYSTEM

© Ray Johnson. Reprinted with permission.   RAY JOHNSON

Whenever humans interact, emotional and physical processes happen. Human interactions are full of information and are mutually influencing. With a systems approach, we "see" the *interactions* that take place, the *information* that is exchanged, and the *influence* that is reciprocally reinforced. Let us look at each of these elements, beginning with interaction.

Example: The biblical prophets urged their audiences to love God with all their heart, mind, and strength. Mind, heart, and strength are three parts of a whole. Love is comprehensive. If you love God only with your mind (cognitive) and do not love God with your heart (devotion, compassion) and your strength (commitment), your love is incomplete.

Example: We believe that body, mind, and spirit encompass the whole person. If, for instance, you become ill and attend solely to your physical symptoms, you are not thinking holistically. You are acting as if neither your mind nor your spirit has anything to do with your sickness. And yet we know that certain feelings (depression, fear) and mental states (excessive worry) can affect bodily processes. "Heavy thoughts bring on physical maladies," Martin Luther remarks. "When the soul is oppressed so is the body." Spirit, too, plays a role in health care. "Hope itself," physician and author Lewis Thomas notes, "is a kind of medicine."[2] Health embraces the whole person.

Example: As a member of a congregation, I attend to needs of my own, of other members, and of people beyond the local setting. If I concentrate on my own needs to the exclusion of others (near or far away), I am not thinking in terms of the whole. I am not contributing to congregational health but rather to an imbalance. I disregard the needs of others. "Contribute to the needs of the saints," the apostle Paul urges, "extend hospitality to strangers" (Romans 12:13).

A Wider View

"The big news of the twenty-first century," Norman Cousins states, "will be that the world as a whole has got to be managed,

not just its parts."[3] We are beginning to see that the whole of
society is connected to the waters, the land, the forests, and
the atmosphere. There is an "ecosystem." Beneath the surface
of things is an invisible connectedness. "Everything in nature
contains all the powers of nature," Ralph Waldo Emerson once
said. "Every thing is made of one hidden stuff."

We will be looking at managing the health (wholeness)
of a congregation. We will be conceiving of the congregation
as a living system or organism—a network of connection and
contact. Thinking in terms of the whole organizes our understanding in a new way and shifts the way we approach and deal
with life. What, then is "holistic" or "systemic" thinking? How
can it inform and shape the way we manage life together in a
congregation?

The word *whole* implies that there are parts and the parts
are connected. Wholeness is not to be confused with oneness.
Wholeness is not about seamlessness; wholeness is not sameness.
Wholeness means two or more parts are interconnected. No
single element of the whole is thought of as functioning inde-
pendently of the other components. Wholeness is relational. In
wholeness differences are not eliminated; rather, they become
alive. The different parts interact and cooperate. Wholeness
involves various parts coming together and interacting.[4]

From Atoms to Galaxies

A system is a collection of parts that connect and interact. Systems range from the cellular to the solar, from an auto's cool-
ing system to the city's transit system, from genes to groups.
The bits and pieces by themselves tell us little about a system's
functioning. We need to see how the bits and pieces act on one
another.

The subatomic level of reality is systemic. Parts interact.
Physicists say that when a particle travels through a vacuum, it
stirs up other particles, which in turn affect the original particle's

path. These tiny particles, called "quanta" (packets of energy), come into being only in relationship to something else. Particles cannot exist as separate things. All quanta are connected. A quantum universe knows nothing of independent particles.

Amazingly, even parts widely separated in time and space can be observed to have a level of connectedness. Could, for example, lunar cycles and psychic moods be related after all? (The word *lunatic* takes its name from the Latin word for "moon," *luna*.) We know that many living things—potatoes, carrots, earthworms, and salamanders—have an "awareness" of the changing phases of sun and moon. Using finely tuned responses to the electro-magnetic influences from these celestial entities, living things adjust their metabolism. Though separated by immense space, potatoes and the moon interact. They are all one of a piece.

At the deepest level of life, reality is interaction. On a more visible plane, interaction is observable in nature. Ornitholo-gist Betty Anne Schreiber and her husband initiated a study of tropical birds in 1979. In 1982 the birds they were studying vanished, except for some embryonic chicks left to starve. The Schreibers were conducting their study during El Niño, the periodic warming of the water in the Pacific off the coasts of Peru and Ecuador. El Niño influences climate around the world. Even a minor change in water temperature affects the direction of the winds, the conditions for a hurricane at sea, and the tor-rential rains that create floods on land. Obviously El Niño had an effect on tropical birds. The logical explanation was that fish had migrated to deeper, colder water. Dependent on the fish, the birds moved to a fresh habitat.

By 1985 the birds, having replenished themselves, return-ed to the original site. But soon again they were gone, several months before the National Weather Service issued a warning that El Niño was impending. The same pattern repeated itself in 1989. The birds, reacting to climatic events, apparently sensed the changes months before sophisticated measurements could confirm them. In the intriguing example of El Niño, we see that the birds, the winds, and the elements of the sea are all of a piece.

Emotional Environments

Everything alive lives in some sort of environment and interacts with it. For people an important part of any environment is other people. We affect them; they affect us. For example, emotions are not simply subjective. They are always expressed in relation to someone or something. We are afraid of someone. We are delighted with an individual. We grieve over the loss of a person. We are angry with a specific group of people. Further, we are aware of how some individuals brighten our spirits by their presence. When we are in the company of others, however, our spirits are darkened.

We tend to assume that individuals live with a fixed nature or according to a personality type. But we do not always act in concert with our nature or type. We live in emotional environments that influence our functioning. We do not act merely on the basis of a personality type. In fact, we may show many different properties, depending on our context. Change the position of people in a system, and they will function differently. Change their functioning, and they will appear to have different natures. In emotional environments, people don't live by their nature alone.

If we place a number of highly predictable people together, they will interact in entirely unforeseeable and complex ways. The whole of their interaction is more than the sum of the parts. The whole will be a multiple of all the emotional interactions. As quanta are defined not by themselves but in relationship to other particles, so too we are never independent of others. We live in emotional environments.

When we think of the congregation as a system or a whole, we also consider all of the interactions of the parts—and the emotional environment in which those interactions take place. What interactions most support health? What emotional interactions most encourage disease process? Is the emotional environment leading toward health or illness?

Getting Looped Together

In a system, information is always exchanged. Loops in every system carry information from one part to another. The more complex a system, the greater the number of loops. A system loves loops. Most biological systems have processes that end up where they started. The circulation of blood, the beat of the heart, food transmuted into energy, and migration are loops of living systems.

Some loops use information to *regulate*. They keep the system in balance. Oxygen, for instance, is held constant by feedback loops. The amount of oxygen in the air is not haphazard. The whole earth regulates the amount with precision. If the atmosphere contained a few percentage points more oxygen than the present level, the forests would incinerate themselves. A few less, and life would suffocate. The level of carbon dioxide is also established at an optimal amount. At higher levels, life on earth would be impossible.

Some loops use information to *amplify*. They create change in the system. Because we are warm-blooded, our temperature control is set around 98.6 degrees. If the body temperature falls below the norm, the body sends out information to increase the temperature. Consequently the body burns food faster, increasing body heat. We shiver, our muscles are more active, creating even more heat. Our brain picks up the "cold" message. We search for a warm room perhaps retrieving a hot drink. We apply heavier clothing to our bodies. If we become too warm, we begin to perspire. We reduce our activity, look for a shady spot, and swallow an ice cold drink.

The "body politic," as well as the body, uses loops for information. The United States constitution provides a set of checks and balances through three loops of government—the executive, the congressional, and the judicial. Each branch carries information that regulates how people live together.

In a congregation, the defeat of a proposal to expand the staff is a loop of regulation. The old balance is retained. Change is negated. If, however, a congregation chooses to build an addition onto its existing facility, information loops carry an amplifying message. There is change.

Both kinds of loops carry information. One keeps the lid on, and the other takes the lid off. One loop ensures stability, the other initiates disturbance. For a system to be healthy, information must flow through both types of loops. Someone has said that disease is a result of information blockage. Information connects the many parts of the body. One part will send "aid" to a damaged part. But if information about the damage is not received, the helping cells of the body will not know to send relief In fact, when cells are under attack from germs, the cells of the body make more connections. The loops supply information, tying the parts together.

In healthy congregations information flows freely. Cells connect with cells. "Rejoice with those who rejoice," St. Paul encourages, "weep with those who weep" (Romans 12:15). Throughout the New Testament, St. Paul uses the phrase "one another": "We are members of one another" (Ephesians 4:25); "…build one another up" (1 Thessalonians 5:11 RSV), and"…love one another" (1 John 4:7). This is an organic view of the church, of cell working with cell to ensure wholeness.

Under the Influence

In a system, there is always a field of *influence*. Effect runs back and forth. Everything modifies or is modified when parts connect. At one time psychiatrist David Spiegel was a strong opponent of the idea that emotions and meanings could influence the course of cancer. He did not believe the "mind" could influence "matter." He set out to prove that a sense of purpose and a specific emotional state could not affect bodily processes. He gathered about ninety women who had metastatic breast cancer. All of them had been treated with conventional therapy, such as radiation and surgery. Half of the women came together once a week for a year to share their feelings in group therapy sessions. These women discussed what it was like to have metastatic breast cancer and fundamentally to be in their situation. When Dr. Spiegel scanned the survival data a decade later, he was flabbergasted. He discovered that the women who came together weekly to share meanings and feelings lived twice as long following their diagnosis as the women who had only conventional treatment.[5]

Researchers in Connecticut divided nursing home residents into two groups matched for ill health and disability. Both groups received amenities beyond the nursing home's usual fare—special meals and entertainment, along with a bedside plant. One group could make choices about a variety of things; the other could not. Group A could choose either an omelet or scrambled eggs for breakfast. Group B had omelets and scrambled eggs on a set schedule. Group A could also choose to sign up to attend special movie nights. But Group B was instructed when to go to the movies. Group A chose how to care for their bedside plants. Group B residents were told how to do it. Only three weeks passed before Group A residents clearly showed evidence of improved health. After eighteen months only half as many of the patients in Group A had died as in Group B.[6] The capacity to influence our environment strengthens our health.

As a system, a congregation influences its own health. By taking responsible action, it shapes its destiny. Whatever a congregation faces— changes, tensions, transitions—those events never tell the whole story. Influence is reciprocal. Yet not all conditions and forces can be controlled. A congregation must manage whatever it can shape and not be overwhelmed by what it cannot. Former basketball coach John Wooden remarked that we should not let what we cannot do overrule what we can do.

A Comparison of Two Ways of Thinking:
Separate Parts and the System

Separate Parts Thinking	System Thinking
Atomistic	Holistic
Problems belong to the individual	Problems belong to the system
Problems are intra (within a part)	Problems are inter (between parts)
Whole can be understood by reduction into parts	Whole can be understood by interaction of the parts
Parts explain the whole	Whole explains parts

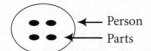

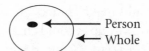

Understanding comes from breaking down into smaller and smaller pieces	Understanding comes from looking up (larger and larger wholes)

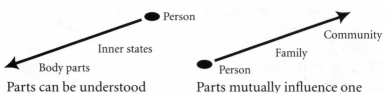

Parts can be understood in themselves	Parts mutually influence one another
Think in lines	Think in loops
A—B—C—D	$A \longleftarrow B$ $\downarrow \nearrow \downarrow$ $C \longleftarrow D$
Cause and effect thinking	Co-causal

A systems approach attends to the impact of relationships on human functioning. In this book, the unit of health or illness is the congregation, and we will examine how we think about congregations and how relationships affect their functioning. *A healthy congregation is one that actively and responsibly addresses or heals its disturbances, not one with an absence of troubles.*

For Reflection and Discussion

1. Describe a system in your home. What interdependent relationships exist?
2. Describe a system in your family. What interdependent relationships exist?
3. Describe a situation in your congregation in which a "loop of regulation" (page 9) was evident. What were the outcomes of this situation?
4. Describe a situation in your congregation in which a "loop of amplification" (page 9) was evident. What were the outcomes of this situation?
5. You may work through this activity on your own. If you are working with a discussion group, however, lead the group through the following steps.

   • Ask group members each to name a problem, challenge, or need facing your congregation. Record the responses on newsprint.
   • Divide the discussion group into subgroups of four or five. Ask each subgroup to select one of the recorded items and to write a sentence that briefly but specifically describes the situation. For example:

   Item: Need to increase involvement in adult education.
   Sentence: The congregation's adult education program involves only 11 percent of the adult members.

- Ask each subgroup to address the situation in two ways.

First, think about the separate parts of the situation. Then think about the situation from a systems perspective. (See pages 11–13.)

Separate-Parts Thinking   **System Thinking**

People are too busy to attend adult classes.

People are busy today. What can we do in adult education programming to deal with this phenomenon?

- Ask each subgroup to report their responses to the large group. After all the responses have been recorded, as a large group discuss the differences between the two approaches.

6. When change in one part of a relationship produces change in other parts of the relationship, you know you are dealing with a system. A mobile is an excellent illustration of a system. What changes in one part of your congregational system have resulted in changes in other parts? What parts were affected most? Why?

Chapter 2

Ten Principles of Health

The analogy between a city undergoing disintegration and a diseased organism does not stretch the imagination too far.
                                            —*Lewis Thomas*

At first sight, it is odd that the laws governing life's responses at such different levels as a cell, a whole person, or even a nation should be so essentially similar.
                                            —*Hans Selye*

Human society is a group of biological organisms and is a biological organism in its own right.
                                            —*Gregory Bateson*

After all, organizations, as the very word declares, are organic, just as corporations, from corpus, are living bodies.
                                            —*James Hillman*

We are developing a perspective for the meaning of health and have started with the understanding of health as wholeness. Now we advance ten principles about health as wholeness.[1] We also begin to look at the meaning of health for a congregation.

Ten Principles of Health and Disease

1. Wholeness is not attainable. (But it can be approximated.)
2. Illness is the necessary complement to health. (It is all right to be sick, feel burdened, and be down.)
3. The body has innate healing abilities. (No one can give you—or the congregation—what you don't already have.)

15

4. Agents of disease are not causes of disease. (All disease processes are enabled.)

5. All illness is biopsychosocial. (Wow! Everything is connected.)

6. The subtle precedes the gross. (Early detection is the best treatment.)

7. Every body is different. (There's no universal treatment for every organism—or congregation.)

8. A healthy circulatory system is the keystone of health and healing. (Feedback systems promote health.)

9. Breathing properly is nourishing to the whole body. (The Spirit must be active among the members of the body of Christ.)

10. The brain is the largest secreting organ of the body, the health maintenance organization (HMO) of the body. (The mind converts ideas into biochemical realities.)

Wholeness Is Not Attainable

Health is a dynamic balance. The human body is always working to maintain a balance in its chemistry and in the functioning of its many parts. French physiologist Claude Bernard talked about the *milieu interieur*, the "interior environment": When out of balance, the body will work to restore balance. An American counterpart, Walter Cannon, referred to *homeostasis*, the capacity of the body to keep its internal environment steady.[2] If agitated, an organism seeks stability. If injured, an organism deploys resources to the damaged spot. If out of balance (such as low on fluids and salts), an organism corrects the imbalance. Homeostasis is cooperative behavior. It is cell-to-cell communication; it is cell working with cell.

Health occurs when the body's systems run smoothly and energy circulates freely. But the balancing act of health is temporary. Wholeness is not achievable in an imperfect world. Health will vary over time. Nonetheless, the drive toward health is the surest tendency in life. Healing is a universal element of all creation, though there are limits to its powers.

"The health of an organization," business executive and author Max DePree writes, "is fragile."[3] Like an organism, an organization must adapt to disturbances and challenges to its balance. Both organisms and organizations are more apt to become sick after major losses, disruptive events, and prominent changes. All put stress on a system's balance. Congregations seek wholeness. But life is incomplete: "Now I know only in part" (1 Corinthians 13:12). Health is not attainable. "If you find the perfect parish," a cleric said, 'join it immediately. But remember," he added, "once you join it, it is no longer perfect." Many of us want to find the perfect or ideal congregation. Because of human folly and sin, however, no one ever will. Still, every congregation can promote its well-being.

Illness Is a Necessary Complement to Health

It is all right to be sick. Illness and health are not opposites. They are complements. We need not view disease as something that should not happen nor interpret it as a sign of weakness. Illness is necessary to health, though illness does not guarantee health. A vaccination is an insertion of a weak, tired virus into the body. We suffer a "mini-disease." As a result, though, the capacities of the immune system are aroused and established. If the body's balance were never tested by disease, it would never develop the immune system, the built-in biochemical defense against infection and disease in the body. The immune system surveys the body to weed out foreign cells. It recognizes what belongs to the body itself and what is alien to it. Every cell belonging to the body has "proof of identity." When invaded by imported cells, the body sounds an alert: "Foreigners!" It quickly mobilizes to defeat them.

Organizations face forces that are "alien" to their integrity or mission. They too need immune capacities. To diminish or

eliminate "alien" forces, the community will undergo a conflict.
The conflict is inevitable, even essential, if resistance resources are
to emerge. Surviving a disaster or crisis may evoke creativity. A
community may strengthen or reexamine its sense of purpose.

At workshops I conduct on healthy congregations, I ask
congregational leaders if they believe their congregations are
healthier now than five years ago. Usually two-thirds of the
participants say yes. Their answers are basically alike: we met
a challenge; we stretched our resources; we examined what we
were doing and changed course; we redefined our problems as
opportunities. Health is 10 percent what happens and 90 percent
how we respond.

The Body Has Innate Healing Abilities

The body possesses an "internal doctor"; it has "internal medicine." Healing always uses the resources of the healing person.
Healing is self-regeneration. It comes from inside, not outside.
Healing is the natural attempt to restore wholeness when wholeness is lost. Physicians, medicine, and surgery do not heal. All
can hasten the healing process or remove obstructions to it. But
healing cannot be obtained from anyone or anything external.
There are no magic bullets.

The healing capacities of the body are operating continu-
ously. Regeneration is the most fundamental feature of living
organisms. Internally each body part has its own renewal rate:
the lining of the stomach renews in a week; skin, in a month;
the liver, in six weeks. We regenerate our blood and our spirit.
Health is an internal, ongoing process. There are no quick fixes
obtained from anyone or anything external.

A congregation may carry the delusional hope that something outside itself will save it. In fact, I have seen many congregations place their well-being in the hands of a magical helper,
an instant solution, or a sure-fire programmatic cure. Looking
outside for help may be a forfeiture of responsibility. Wanting

to be taken care of simply compounds the illness. Helplessness is a disease in itself. Congregations need to see themselves as the source of their own healing. The power to heal is internal.

Sometimes outside help is necessary—and healthy. The congregation is stuck. An effective outside source of help will not support dependency. Rather, it will help the congregation to build the inner resources that can stabilize life together and produce a more adequate organization for the future.

Agents of Disease Are Not Causes of Disease

By themselves, pathogens are not able to induce sickness. All pathogens need a host cell to arouse the disease process. Viruses, for example, wait their chance to do their mischief in our bodies. Many are particular about which cell type they will infect and when. Viruses treat a living cell as a meal. But disease is a transaction between the invading microbe and the condition of the person. Claude Bernard said the microorganism is like a "seed" that will only sprout into disease if the "soil" is too weak to resist it.[4] Disease is essentially the result of the host's response to the virus. All disease processes are enabled. Strengthening the resistance of the host cells is paramount in treatment, rather than simply focusing on disease agents and counteracting them.

In life together, when there is an effect people do not like, they become anxious. They normally focus on a single cause or culprit. But as in an organism, "bugs" alone do not cause disease in organizations. All anxiety needs a host cell, a co-contributor. We easily overlook how two sides give rise to and maintain a problem through mutual functioning.

I recall working with a Midwestern congregation. The leaders complained about Erik Schmidt. Whenever the leaders wanted to implement something new, Erik Schmidt protested. It couldn't be done; it would be a waste of money—whatever. And then, when they did manage to override Schmidt's objections, he would notify them that the undertaking wasn't sufficient or done properly. I said to the leaders that they were being "Schmidt-ed on." In order, however, to have a "Schmidting process," there needed to be a virus (Schmidt) *and* a host cell (Schmidtees). The president of the church council said to me, wryly, "Are you saying that Schmidt happens?"

All Illness Is Biopsychosocial

Health is a mysterious mix of factors and conditions. We are mind-bodies in environments. Health is a power-sharing arrangement between physiology, pathology, psychology, emotional history, social context, doctors and nurses, and medicine. Emotions can trigger potent bodily secretions that affect blood chemistry, heart rate, and the activity of the immune system. Cardiologist James Lynch claims that "almost every cause of death is significantly influenced by human companionship."[5] Studies show that economic recession is followed by increases in death from nearly all causes.

Internally, the same power sharing arrangement enhances health. All healthy cells, for example, have the capacity to be interdependent, to "die" for the sake of other cells. Further, the immune system is a "team player." It connects to the neurological, endocrine, and nervous systems, constantly exchanging information. Within the nervous system, no part is capable of acting without affecting and being affected by other parts.

Essayist and poet Wendell Berry takes the idea of health as wholeness, parts interacting, even further. The whole problem of health in soil, plant, animal, and humanity, Berry contends is one great subject. "I believe," he adds, "that the community—in the fullest sense: a place and all its creatures—is the smallest unit of health and that to speak of the health of an isolated individual is a contradiction in terms."[6]

The health of a congregation is multifaceted. It is a power-sharing arrangement. Attitudes count. Working together counts. Faithfulness matters. Mood and tone are significant.

For example, Hans Selye, a pioneer in charting the effect of emotional states on physical health, notes that the two emotions most detrimental to health are vengeance and bitterness. Conversely, the most nourishing attitude is gratitude.[7] Healthy congregations certainly foster a caring spirit and encourage a confident tone. At the heart of congregational life is the Gospel of Christ's steadfast love, given in God's Word and Sacraments. Healthy congregations are spirited. They are graced and gracious, generous with each other and outsiders. They are communities of thanks and praise. They are wholesome and refreshing.

The Subtle Precedes the Gross

Short of prevention, early treatment is the best treatment. Everything in creation starts small and grows, including conditions of disease. Early warnings come from small disturbances. When disturbances are still local and small, they are more treatable. Their peak is not so high; their duration is not so long. The deeper into its course a disease proceeds, the stronger the means needed to stifle or reverse it.

Congregations, no less than individuals, are subject to the same principle. If a problem or conflict is allowed to fester and swell, it becomes even more embedded and resistant to management. Generally, congregations refuse to act on early warning signals. Some are fearful of emotional outbreaks, financial troubles, and loss of members. They remain "numb to signals" that something is amiss. Waiting too long only gives the disease process more time to become entrenched.

Everybody Is Different

Individual differences are common. People are biochemically unique. People's responses to drugs and foods vary. Universal applicability of any one form of treatment is not possible. One person's medicine can be another's poison.

There are more than 350,000 congregations in America, and it is difficult to define what is normal for all. Certainly congregations share many functions and purposes. Each congregation, however, has its own nuances, particularities, special stories, fitting moments, and historical twists and turns. No remedy will necessarily address every congregation's issues. What is best for congregation A might not be best for congregation B, and might not even be best for congregation A two years from now.

Breathing Properly Is Nourishing to the Whole Body

Breathing is a vital function of health. To survive, the cells of the body need the oxygen breath supplies. Full, deep, expansion of the lungs brings nourishment to the central nervous system. Not surprisingly, *breath* has been hewn from the same word as *spirit* in many languages. At one time the soul was believed to be located in the diaphragm.

Remember how the spirit hovered over the chaos in Genesis 1. Balance came out of disorder. Remember how Jesus is pictured in John's gospel as having "breathed" on the apostles. And then he gave them authority concerning that special healing, to forgive sins in his name. The Spirit of God and the spirit of the people nourish congregational life. In fact, in the Gospel of John, Jesus refers to the Spirit as the "comforter" (John 14:16, 26 KJV), meaning literally "with strength" (*cum forte*). The promise of the Spirit is strengthening and emboldening to the whole congregation.

The Brain Is the Largest Secreting Organ of the Body, the Health Maintenance Organization (HMO) of the Body

The brain has the power to regulate all bodily functions. All organs are autonomous in function but regulated by and in communication with the brain. Being more a pharmacy than a computer, the brain uses dozens of chemical messages in its far-reaching influence. The messengers are called neuropeptides or neurotransmitters. They hook up the brain with the nervous system, endocrine system, and the immune system. The outcome is a web humming with information, touching the life of every cell.

The brain is the most prolific gland in the body. Using its secretions in different combinations, the brain "writes" thousands of prescriptions to meet the body's needs. Someone calls the brain the "magnificent apothecary." Some of the secretions—endorphins—are actually biological acts of mercy. They serve as painkillers. Besides reducing pain, the brain activates other health measures, specifically increasing the number of disease fighting immune cells. Robert Ornstein, noted author of books about the brain, states, "To understand health is to understand the continual role of the brain in maintaining the resistance of the body."[8]

Comparable to the brain's functioning in the body is the functioning of the leaders in the congregation. They are in the position to influence the emotional field in far reaching ways. A healthy body relies on proper channels from the brain to the body parts as well as commitment from individual cells to do the will of the head. A similar arrangement is found in healthy organizations between leaders and followers.

For Reflection and Discussion

1. Review the list of ten principles of health and disease (pages 15–16). Again, you may work through this activity on your own. Or lead a discussion group through the following steps.

   • Divide the large group in half. Ask group A to focus on the odd-numbered principles; group B, on the even numbered.

- Ask each group to describe what each principle means for the well-being of your congregation.
- Invite each group to report their insights. Allow the other group to respond and ask questions.

2. If you are working with a group, divide the group into subgroups of four or five. Ask each subgroup to write an eleventh principle. Record these principles on newsprint. Then invite the large group to discuss each principle.
3. Refer to the discussion of principle 10 on pages 22–23. Who is the "brain" of the congregation? How is this expressed?

Chapter 3

Promoting Healthy Congregations

Today research indicates that the way people cope with incipient illness may be at least as important as the biological pathogens themselves in determining health or illness.
— *Kenneth Pelletier*

Getting well may be less a matter of fighting illness than of counterbalancing it with the healthy aspects of our lives.
— *Marc Ian Barasch*

It is more important to know what sort of patient has the disease than what sort of disease the patient has.
— *Sir William Osler*

The healing system is the way the body mobilizes all its resources to combat disease. The belief system is often the activator of the healing system.
— *Norman Cousins*

A Tale of Three Cities

First Church is barely keeping its balance. Membership is static. Financial giving is slightly better than it was the last two years, but each year it is more difficult to find leaders and workers. A longtime lay leader observes, "More members want the congregation to meet their needs. They are less interested in contributing to something beyond themselves."

Is this a healthy congregation? Or is it showing symptoms of disease?

Trinity Church is bleeding. From the early 1960s to the early 1990s, its membership declined from 1,800 to 1,200. But strangely, its school has maintained steady enrollment figures. At one time, the students were white and primarily from the congregation. Now, 90 percent are non-members, and 80 percent are multicultural.

Many of Trinity's former members moved to suburbs farther from the city. In the next ten years, Trinity will likely lose another 200 members. "It took us several years to recognize what was happening to our neighborhood," the associate pastor says. "Then we spent several more years making changes. We had to change from simply receiving new members to moving out into the community to seek members."

Is Trinity healthy? Is it possible for a congregation to be vital when it is doing less today than yesterday?

Community Church is thriving. It is only eight years old and already in its third building program. Staff members bristle with ideas for new programs. Limited space for further expansion is the only apparent impediment to the church's continued rapid growth. Some members are discussing capping membership at about two thousand unless new property is obtained. Although real estate costs are exploding, another group of members is aggressively seeking new property to purchase. This group fears a loss of momentum if the congregation fails to relocate. The church staff is divided about which direction to take. The minister of music believes the staff is burdened with too much work and the congregation with too much debt. "The only limit we face," the minister of evangelism counters, "is ourselves."

Is there potential for disease at Community? Are the emerging differences of opinion symptoms of a deeper disturbance?

Both Kingdoms

"Everyone who is born holds dual citizenship, in the kingdom of the well and the kingdom of the sick," Susan Sontag notes.

"Although we prefer to use only the good passport, sooner or later each of us is obliged, at least for a spell, to identify ourselves as citizens of that other place."[1] Potentially, congregations can be members of both kingdoms. Health is a process, not a thing or state. It is ongoing, dynamic, and ever changing. Health is a direction, not a destination, a once-and-for-all property.

Community Church faces a threat. Its primary need is to have all its parts working together. The question is, can Community reconcile its sharp differences about how to handle growth? No congregation can serve two visions. It needs a clear direction.

Shared vision is necessary, but some differences can coexist as long as members are loyal to Christ, the head of the body, and each cares for the other. Some individuals, however, feel threatened by the disorder differences create. They confuse community with sameness. They may even make their own experience, perception, or way a law for others. But no body can remain healthy if its cells are selfish or not in touch with other, different cells, or if the body insists that all cells be alike. Learning how to deal with the threat differences arouse is a task of healthy living.

First Church is at a plateau. It is not growing, and many of its members do not see a mission beyond serving the members' needs. If First devotes time to diagnosis and weakness, it will not stay healthy. Health is always about attitudes, moods, and choices. The leaders of First must be careful not to generate a negative tone, even though the number of active participants is declining. They need a new confidence. They need to help members to see that individual needs are tied to the needs of everyone. The mood and tone of leadership is significant because morale flows down.

The Aeolian Chamber Music Company of New York City had its private and federal funding support cut back. When a reporter for the New York Times asked the director of the music group whether this would affect his group, he responded, "Only financially." This kind of thinking benefits the health of a group.

The feeling of panic does not control people. Helping people manage their disturbing feelings is a form of disease prevention. Our own self-control is preventive as well.

The third congregation—Trinity—stays healthy despite declining membership. It is learning how to respond as its old ways of functioning are challenged. It is adapting in ways that keep its vision in focus. Trinity can do little about changes in its environment. But its leaders are specific about their responses to the changes.

Health Promoters

Congregational leaders are the key stewards of the congregation as a unit in itself. They, by virtue of their positions in the system, can most promote congregational health. More important to First, Trinity, or Community congregations than any of the conditions they face is the capacity of their leaders to make clear and effective responses to the conditions. On what specific items or forces, then, will they need to focus in order to impact the health of their respective congregations? What generally influences congregational health? We will examine seven health promoters—purpose, appraisal and management of conflict, clarity, mood and tone, mature interaction, healing capacities, and a focus on resources.

Sense of Purpose

The human body is a purposeful organization. The body's parts must function in balance to preserve its very existence. Its surest tendency is to move toward health.

Healthy congregations are also purposeful organizations. They have a clear direction. They keep asking, what is God calling us to be? What is the meaning of what we do? They have a working vision that conveys the message that together they can influence their future. Vision always requires revision. Health is a continuous process, and healthy congregations keep at the work of visioning and revisioning.

"If your line of vision is even with the floor," professor Leland Kaiser says, "you can starve to death in a full pantry."[2] The vision needs to be realistic yet challenging. People will hesitate to follow leaders who avoid stressful conditions and will not take clear action. Leaders create conditions that make something new possible.

Appraise and Manage Conflict

Healthy congregations use their resources and strengths to manage conflict. They do not let conflict fester. They have the wisdom to face the tensions and stresses that befall all living systems.

The work of one researcher unravels some of the mystery of health.[3] Medical sociologist Aaron Antonovsky puzzled over a study showing that about 75 percent of disease affects 25 percent of the population. If microorganisms cause disease, he thought, would disease not be more evenly distributed? He believed other factors had to be involved.

In another study comparing 77 women who survived the Nazi death camps with 210 who had not, Antonovsky discovered that 51 percent of the control group and 29 percent of the survivors were in good overall emotional and physical health. The survivors functioned well, raising families, working, having friends, and taking part in community activity. They experienced the incredible horror and degradation of the camps, followed by years of displacement, and yet were in reasonable health. Antonovsky reasoned that more than stress itself had to generate disease.

In a third study he found 587 chronically asthmatic patients who were discharged from hospitals. Researchers predicted which of them would be readmitted to the hospital within six months based on their medical history. Of those predicted to be rehospitalized, only 32 percent were actually readmitted. Past illnesses could not alone predict future sickness.

Antonovsky saw that neither germs nor stress, and not even medical history—separately or together—led to illness. After years of research, he came up with a missing ingredient. He called it the "sense of coherence." It is a disposition or orientation to life: all the parts of one's life are connected, something ties all people together, and life coheres in a meaningful way. This sense of coherence gives people a compass, builds confidence that things will work out, and contributes to belief that the person can positively influence the outcome.

Antonovsky claimed that a "sense of coherence" could be a "group property" as well as an individual strength. It can be as instrumental in the health of a community as an individual. Collective stressors are as real as personal ones. Social entities engage threats to their health in the same ways people do. In a congregation, collective stressors might include *major life changes*, such as:

- departure of a longtime pastor
- mismanagement of financial resources
- clergy sexually acting out
- new building program
- forced resignation of staff member
- steady loss in membership
- downturn in financial contributions
- important changes in the lives of leaders
- intense staff conflict
- catastrophe destroying physical facilities
- informal, nagging complaints
- sudden, violent death of children
- economic depression in the larger community
- rift between congregation and judicatory
- group of members leaving congregation

Other collective stressors might include *chronic conditions*, such as:

- decision making residing in the hands of a few people
- griping as a normative way of behavior
- pastor dominating almost every aspect of congregational life
- little accountability
- perennial shortage of money
- nothing really getting done
- a sense of boredom or depression
- feeling of hopelessness
- small group dominating
- differences ignored and not discussed
- "viruses" (secrets, blame, and so forth) enabled
- poor or inadequate facilities

Antonovsky found that a "sense of coherence" is a major determinant of a group's, as well as an individual's, ability to move toward or to maintain health. Three interrelated parts compose a "sense of coherence":

Meaningfulness: A congregation has an overall sense of purpose. The people are willing to take up a challenge. Because life matters, they involve themselves in what is done. They make a commitment because a situation is worthy of investment. They believe the outcome of their response is of value.

Manageability: A congregation has a sense of control, a sense of being able to influence events. The people believe they can, as far as possible, shape their destiny. They believe the resources are available to act effectively. They believe their response will lead to valued outcome.

Comprehensibility: A congregation judges reality soundly. Knowing there is little danger in viewing the world as a challenge, they must make sense of confusion and change. They use information as a stimulus for growth. They believe the valued outcome will be health promoting.

A high sense of coherence helps people to appraise tension more realistically and less anxiously. It allows people to make more resourceful responses to challenges and stressors.

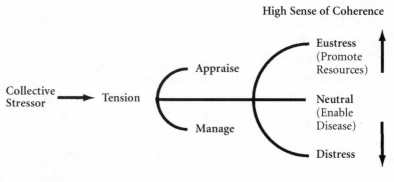

In the diagram above a "collective stressor" arouses tension in a congregation. The excitation carries twin possibilities, either eustress (promoting health) or distress (enabling disease). A strong sense of coherence affects how the tension is appraised and handled in favor of eustress. A low sense of coherence leads in the direction of great distress.

A strong sense of coherence motivates people to be active, focused, and imaginative in their responses to tension. A low sense of coherence paralyzes people, and their responses are diffuse or unclear. They do not act decisively.

Clarity

One thing the physical body is quite clear about is what is self and what is not self. The entire immune system devotes itself to preserving the body's integrity. Likewise, healthy congregations are always working on clarity, whether clarity of beliefs, direction, or responsibility.

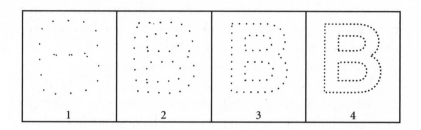

In the above diagram, you see how the figure B sharpens as you move from panel 1 to panel 4. Healthier congregations will work for concreteness and specificity. In fact, what often permits a virus to become opportunistic and to infect a living cell is its capacity to "hide" its protein surface. The virus disguises itself. The immune response cannot detect its real essence. That is what happens with strains of influenza. They change their "protein coats."

Healthy congregations are clear about what is and what is not beneficial to their well-being. Less healthy congregations will allow more fuzziness, indecisiveness, vagueness, and secrets or disguises. Healthy congregations stay healthy because their immune responses are clear and direct. The immune system keeps integrity intact.

Imagine, for instance, that you are looking at slides or a movie. Everything is out of focus. It will not be long before you become angry, confused, or disinterested. Clarity keeps people's attention and mobilizes their energy.

Mood and Tone

Moods, attitudes, beliefs, and feelings can affect the body. Mind moves matter. Consciousness interacts with cells. Mood and tone affect organizations as well. Better functioning congregations are more energized. Their interactions are charged with spontaneity, intensity, and wholehearted involvement. Less healthy congregations appear "stuck," less energized, permeated with a depressive mood, and pessimistic in outlook. Unlike the healthy congregation, a less healthy one exhibits fewer signs of hope, minimal chances to be playful, and little regard for the future.

The word *illness* comes from the Latin word *ensatus*. It is a picture word; it means literally not having one's elbows aligned. Instead of being in a relaxed position or having handles to hold things in balance, a person is neither relaxed nor balanced. In like manner, less healthy congregations are more rigid, imbalanced, or lacking in elbow room. They do not have the flexibility to bend and flow.

Mature Interaction

The body, being a part of nature, needs time. It participates in seasons, rhythms, and growth processes. Indeed, the body functions more like a garden than a machine, though the opposite is commonly believed.

Organizations, too, function well when they attend to growth processes. In a systems approach, the growth process that receives major attention is the person's capacity to be a self in a relationship system—to grow as a mature person. One of the great tasks of leaders is to foster such growth. Author Robert Greenleaf, known for the concept of "servant-leader," observes, "The best test, and difficult to administer is, Do those served grow as persons? Do they, while being served, become healthier, wiser, freer, more autonomous, more likely themselves to become servants?"[4] Healthy congregations are obviously invested in the growth of people. They are not devoted to how people failed or who is to blame. If invested in growth, healthy congregations will have leaders devoted to learning.

In the following diagrams, you see the healthy and unhealthy congregation contrasted. In figure 1 the leaders function in such a way that over a period of time people are more able to meet their own needs. They are good stewards of their lives.

Figure 1

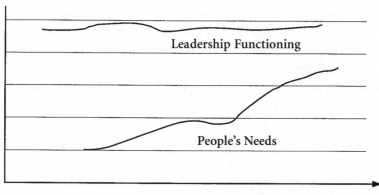

Time

In figure 2, however, the leaders' functioning decreases and the people remain more dependent. Both leaders and group members function at lower levels. Growth is impeded. This is what often happens in less than healthy congregations. The leaders protect or rescue people; the people expect to be protected or rescued. No one grows because there is no challenge. In place of stewardship, dependency is encouraged.

Figure 2

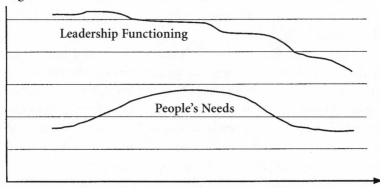

Time

Healing Capacities

Healing is the body's potential to repair and regenerate itself. The body can heal itself because it has a healing system. "Healing is more a process of uncovering what we already possess," writer and television and film producer Marc Ian Barasch notes, "rather than manufacturing a 'better' self."[5]

Congregations have healing capacities. They possess strengths and resources. Healthy congregations are known for renewing and regenerating themselves. Like natural organisms, congregations live through a series of births and deaths, agonies and ecstasies, or ebbs and flows. Living things know no other reality than one in which we suffer and begin again.

Healing and illness processes move from challenge to response back to challenge, from disturbance to regeneration to collapse and back to stability. "The wheel of well-being" on the following page illustrates how a congregation could be at different "places" at different times. The circle indicates that health and illness are processes. The danger is that a congregation might become "stuck" at the disease or acute reaction stages and not use its healing capacities.

What is natural, though, can be hampered by our own meddlesome yet opposite actions—rushing the healing process or retarding it. Some wounds resemble little cuts. They are clean with sharp edges; they are fixed with a bandage, a few sutures, and perhaps a hug and a sympathetic word. With minimal care, the wound heals.

Other wounds are quite different. They are wider and deeper, with jagged edges and debris. No sutures could tie them together and make them tight. This kind of wound has to heal by a process called "granulation." It is a slow process; the healing happens from the inside out. The small pieces of debris must be removed. Sterile solutions wash away grit and dirt foreign to the healing process. Care must be taken to protect the raw, open tissue from further injury. Slowly, the wound heals, becoming smaller and more shallow. Many processes are at work at once. The new skin

The Wheel of Well-Being

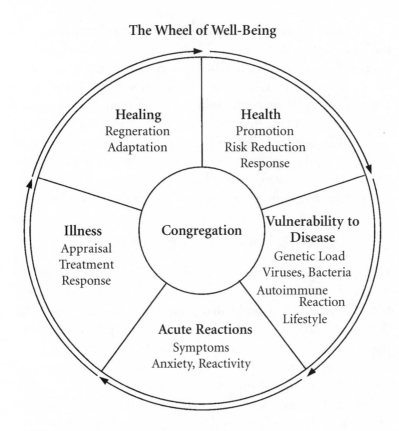

is pink and fresh. As the evidence of the old wound passes away, behold, there is a "new creation."

Sometimes people want to save time or desire a quick fix. They use sutures to bring the offense together tightly, to make the edges fit together. They pull harder. All too often, though, these wounds buckle.

When a wound is prematurely closed, the edges never come together appropriately. The wound festers within, even though it appears to be well. Eventually cells die from infection, lack of oxygen, poor circulation, or isolation. There is no community. The cells do not come together to heal. Then everything starts to erode, and sometimes the disease goes deeper into a bone or blood. There is widespread distortion because healing was forced or coerced, not given time to do its proper work.

At other times people heal too slowly. Paul Brand mentions the "compensation syndrome," in which people who might gain from a disability tend to heal at a slower rate. In a comparison of similar injuries that take place in different settings, Brand notes a measurable difference in healing rates. If there is a payoff, the same injury can take longer to heal.[6]

Healthy congregations will neither anxiously hurry nor slow down the healing process. Because it is a natural force, healing knows its own fitting time. Healthy congregations let their strengths and resources carry them through their woundedness.

A Focus on Resources

Healthy congregations focus on the healing resources, not the disease process. Let me illustrate from the actual experience of First Church. You'll recall that First's membership was static. But more troubling was the shift in people's expectations. More people were looking for their own needs to be met and fewer were expecting to contribute to the same of others. How did the leaders of First Church meet this challenge?

To understand what happened at First Church, the congregation al "genogram" on the following page illustrates how the congregation has functioned since its inception.

First Church has had a history of strong resources: (1) the relationship between pastors and lay leaders has been respectful and effective ever since Rev. Sewell; (2) the way the congregation communicates with its membership is outstanding (Rev. Righter's wife was a "communication specialist," and she set up a communication network, including a parish newsletter that invites regular reading); (3) stewardship has been emphasized and the people respond well.

Not everything has worked well over the years, of course, but now faced with greater expectations, First can promote greater health by focusing on those past resources or by developing potential new ones. A congregation simply cannot remain on the side of health unless it does. A focus on disease, pathology,

Genogram of First Church

Membership Size	Date	Minister	Additions	Deletions	Stressors
	1957	Rev. William Sewell	Church orgazined		
140	1960		New building	Rev. Sewell's wife dies in auto accident	Grief
160	1962		Rev. Sewell marries a divorced woman in congregation		Tension, gossip
	1964			Rev. Sewell leaves and takes new position	Polarization among members
200	1965	Rev. Ken Lovejoy	New pastor		Pastor has major illness problems
	1968		Major growth spurt	Rev. Lovejoy resigns and takes disability	Grief
260	1969	Rev. Hale Righter	New pastor; growth continues		Grief over Rev. Lovejoy's death
390	1975		Building addition; three part-time staff members added		
530	1983			Rev. Righter retires	
510	1985	Rev. Sean Jones	New pastor		
490	1987		Remodeling of old building; new lay leadership		
475	1993				Leaders recognize shift in members' perception

and weakness only cripples its efforts. The focus on strength, options, and resources empowers.

For Reflection and Discussion

1. Review the descriptions of the three congregations (pages 25–26) and the author's commentary on each congregation's situation. What is applicable to your congregation?
2. What "major life changes" and "chronic conditions" (pages 30–31) has your congregation experienced? How have members responded?
3. Construct a genogram (page 39) for your congregation. Make a list of things you have learned from the genogram. What actions might you undertake in response to these learnings?

PART 2

DISEASE PROCESS

Chapter 4

Congregations at Risk

Certainly conflict and power plays go on in church, but
because intimacy is threatened by these realities, we cover them
in hopes of maintaining a facade of peace.

—*Parker Palmer*

Competing pressures tempt one to believe that an issue deferred
is a problem solved; more often it is crisis invented.

—*Henry Kissinger*

You can't defeat helplessness.

—*Salvador Minuchin*

Families, churches, business, and governments become sick by
refusing to face painful realities.

—*M. Scott Peck*

The Core

Congregations are unique and complex. Yet all congregations are working with a small set of core issues:

- *mission* and how to achieve it
- *strengths* and *resources* and how to implement them
- *anxiety* and how to manage it
- *wholeness* and how to maintain it

Struggling ineffectively with one or more of the core issues, congregations can put their health at risk. We will examine four at-risk conditions for congregations:

43

- overfocusing on clergy at the expense of mission
- giving inadequate attention to painful events to the detriment of healing capacities
- adapting to weakness at the cost of integrity
- taking sides and hostages at the expense of the hard tasks of love

When the Pastor Is the Elephant

Six wise men who are blind come across an elephant. Each sage deciphers the animal's shape from a singular vantage point:

> Six wise men of India
> An elephant did find
> And carefully they felt its shape
> (For all of them were blind).
>
> The first he felt towards the tusk,
> "It does to me appear.
> This marvel of an elephant
> Is very like a spear."
>
> The second sensed the creature's side
> Extended flat and tall,
> "Ahah!" he cried and did conclude,
> "This animal's a wall."
>
> The third had reached towards a leg
> And said, "It's clear to me
> What we should all have instead
> This creature's like a tree."
>
> The fourth had come upon the trunk
> Which he did seize, and shake,
> Quoth he, "This so-called elephant
> Is really just a snake."

The fifth had felt the creature's ear
And fingers o'er it ran,
"I have the answer, never fear,
The creature's like a fan!"

The sixth had come upon the tail
As blind he did grope,
"Let my conviction now prevail
This creature's like a rope."

And so these men of missing sight
Each argued loud and long
Though each was partly in the right
They all were in the wrong.[1]

Each focused on one part of the elephant, the wise men cannot encompass the whole. The elephant is believed to be a wall, a tree, and even a rope.

The fable reminds me of what happens when congregations overfocus on their clergy. There are two consequences, neither of which is healthy. First, when overfocused on the pastor, people find it immensely difficult to see the rest of the system. As a result, they are blind to how other forces and people contribute to what is happening. Perspective is distorted. No one part, however, can explain the whole. Second, when a congregation is overfocused on clergy, it cannot keep its focus on its mission. Instead of focusing on who they are and what they are about as a community, they peer intently at who the pastor is and what the pastor does. Again, perspective is skewed. Extreme focus on clergy is similar to putting extra strain on a body part or organ. Collapse, injury, or disease will follow.

The overfocus cuts both ways. Sometimes the extreme attention is a matter of idealizing clergy. At other times the intense preoccupation consists of negative complaining and nagging dissatisfaction. Either way, the focus is riveted on one part of the whole. The congregation has an "elephant" on its hands.

Where's Your Focus?

The chart below contrasts two types of congregations. Think about your own situation. Where does your congregation fit? What in your congregation needs continued support or change?

Clergy-Focused Congregations

1. Excessive focus on clergy (difficult to think of the rest of the system); overinvested in clergy ("hero or goat"); clergy primarily responsible for what happens

2. Dependency encouraged (parent/child arrangement); no activity without clergy present

3. Neediness is enabled

4. Clergy expected to motivate, uplift, or rescue people

5. Inflexible roles (survival depends on a prescribed way of functioning)

6. Cycle of emotional fusion (lack of "distance"; clergy not seen as separate individuals; clergy are "owned")

7. "We" (very few speak for themselves); allow inappropriate behavior to exist, no one confronts or speaks up

Mission-Focused Congregations

1. A clear focus on identity and destiny

2. Stewardship emphasized; responsibility is distributed; interdependence

3. Needs are met without promoting dependency

4. Clergy expected to organize people toward mission

5. Resiliency in functioning

6. Clergy are separate selves; clergy set goals and take stands

7. "I" positions are respected; lots of dialogue (physicist David Bohm says, "Dialogue means not winning points")

8. "Consensus sensitive" (difference is seen as attack, can't survive if we don't agree); clergy is the hub of harmony

8. Vision sensitive (differences are tolerated because vision guides and solidifies people)

9. Disagreement is dangerous (calm surface)

9. Conflict is normal, essential, and managed

10. Closed system (lack of "oxygen," no corrective feedback, novelty is not entertained)

10. Open system (lots of information, new ideas, feedback loops)

© Ray Johnson. Reprinted with permission.

Covenant's Lesson

"Organizations," professor Margaret Wheatley states, "do best when they focus on direction and vision."[2] That is precisely what happens in a mission-focused congregation. In the following story, we encounter, however, a clergy-focused congregation. It is in a state of imbalance. One part of the whole is too much of the whole. Notice, too, how shifting to a mission focus carries a cost. Without disease, a move toward better balance cannot occur.

Covenant Church is only six and a half years old. It has 780 members. Energetic Kent Wallace started the new church with three goals: (1) worship and programs would be high *quality*; (2) there would be an atmosphere of *excitement*; (3) the ministry would be highly *relational*.

Covenant is located in North Shore Lakes, what was once swamp and woods but now is a burgeoning town of shops and homes as well as fast growing churches like Covenant. Certainly quality, excitement, and relationship fit Covenant's context.

About 20 percent of Covenant's current membership had never been associated with a church before. An equal percentage had been members some place else but were minimally active before getting involved at Covenant. These families had great admiration and ardor for Kent's ministry. When several of these people who were leaders suddenly resigned their positions, others became curious and asked questions. They were baffled.

For five months a quiet battle had been emerging. It certainly betrayed the placid, amiable surface of Covenant's life. Not only did the leaders resign, but they also withdrew from worship and activities at the same time. Kent answered the curious, saying, "There's a difference of philosophy. We can't have two directions." The leaders who resigned were more specific: "Pastor cannot let go of the reins. He controls everything." One of them, Betsy, said, "I'm depressed. Kent means so much to me. He brought me into the church. But once you get closer to him, you see this incredible need for power."

Within three months, a second exodus of leaders occurred. Tension hovered over the congregation like a ubiquitous winter cloud. Some relief came when the church board granted Kent a three-month leave of absence.

Many factors play into Covenant's situation. Still, one pattern stands out vividly. From the start, Kent Wallace was the center of everything. He was the focus. Indeed, he served well and the results testified to his efforts. As time went by, the size of the congregation increased, people became interested in assuming roles of leadership, and new forces developed. Kent continued to function as the focal point. He encouraged that role; many people consented to it. The tension between Kent and the leaders grew as Kent saw things slipping away from his grasp. Lay leaders took on the responsibilities he once garnered for himself. For the loyal core to rebel against Kent was just astonishing. Equally amazing, returning from his leave of absence, Kent announced his resignation and said he was seeking another pastoral position.

When I came to consult with Covenant, I encountered a confused and splintered congregation. About fifty people had left, basing their decisions on Kent's departure. Confusion was the rule: "How could we in less than a year go from an enthusiastic group to a moribund collection of souls?"

Betsy, a pediatrician (quoted above), took the chart contrasting a clergy-focused congregation with a mission-focused congregation, glanced at it, and made these comments:

> Kent is a marvelous pastor. He has wonderful talents. I am remorseful over his leaving us. But Covenant has become more than Kent.... Something I think he had trouble understanding, if not accepting. We have been a clergy-focused congregation. Look at this list. I made him my "hero." I was enthralled. I was in a dependent position to him for a while, as were many of us. Look at number 5—inflexible roles. As long as you needed Kent, things were fine. Once you were no longer dependent, things changed with him. Oh, number

7. "We!" For so long, "we" prevailed. Keep the peace. Don't rock the boat. So no one said "I." When a few of us did, pandemonium followed.

Ideally, a congregation is mission focused. All churches are mission focused in part; none is totally focused on mission. Even though *mission* is the heart and soul of a congregation, members can never *assume* it is the focus. Mission must be intentionally designed and continually redesigned.

Wasted Suffering at All Angels

Not paying attention to the signals of physical pain is an at-risk condition. Pain is a teacher without which we cannot live. "Silencing pain without considering its message," Paul Brand says, "is like disconnecting a ringing fire alarm to avoid receiving bad news."[3] In pain's absence, we live in peril. Without the sensation of pain, someone can sit in the same position for long periods, impairing the flow of blood to the joints. If the behavior is repeated, deterioration of the joints is inevitable. Some people do not experience pain and therefore do not know to remove their hands from the heat. Tissue damage can be extensive. We need to experience pain for the sake of health and healing. "People who cannot feel pain," authors Randolph Nesse and George Williams assert, "are nearly all dead by age thirty."[4] Lepers, for example, do not have pain's adaptive capacities. Leprosy destroys pain nerves, leaving the body without sensors. No alarm goes off; pain's message is mute.

If an organization is like an organism, it needs pain as a messenger, as well. Some people, however, have low pain thresholds. They refuse to acknowledge that "collective stressors" exist; they ignore "corporate pain" to achieve false comfort. If these people prevail, blocking the congregation's awareness of pain, the congregation is at risk.

By escaping what is unpleasant, the instruction of pain is wasted. People learn little from their crises. They only risk greater danger in the future. Certainly people look to the congregation to be a place of safety and a source of comfort. Painful situations nullify the safety and comfort. As a rule, however, the body flourishes when challenged by activity, tension, and exercise. Healthy congregations can grow through the challenge of pain. They discover strength in managing it, and they head off many of its negative effects in the process.

"Since the death of Jack, we've never recovered," Danielle Parquet told me. Jack was a longtime member and the music director of All Angels. Six years ago he was murdered. The killer has never been arrested, though many believe the assassin was a coworker at the university where Jack was a professor. Over the course of the ensuing half dozen years, occasional stories leaked out about Jack's harassment of women in the con-gregation—inappropriate touching, phone calls with sexual advances, and public gestures. The "word" was that when confronted with his behavior, Jack said his actions were totally misunderstood.

"Strangely," Danielle continued, "the violence and the mystery of his death has been a nonsubject at All Angels. Total silence." Over the years, Jack had secured a favorable position with many people in the small, urban congregation. He was known as being witty, smart, and "able to talk himself out of anything." The silence seemed unfitting.

"No one really knew anything except for a few," she re-ported, "until a church leader stumbled onto it." What Danielle was referring to involved two $10,000 payments to women in the church who had charged Jack with sexual harassment. In exchange for their silence, a financial agreement was reached. Payments came out of church funds. Once discovered, the payoff was made known. Among the reasons given for the subterfuge was an impending gift from Jack's mother. A wealthy widow in failing health, she had contacted All Angels regarding a memorial gift to honor her only son. The gift would exceed one million dollars, possibly two. Fearful of endangering her gift, the individuals responsible discouraged or minimized "talk" about Jack. Would the stories leak out to the ailing mother? The gift would assuredly guarantee All Angels' survival for years to come.

Danielle sketched out the problem:

> So here we are. Some people suspicious of Jack. Some people angry with Jack. Other so enamored with him that they think no one could take his place. Others hiding the truth about Jack. Some totally ignorant of everything. Different kinds of pain, yet we pretend all is normal. Now we have new pains—distrust, anger, feeling used...

We "waste" suffering if we gloss over, deny, avoid, or neglect its message. At All Angels the pain of uncertainty became joined to the pain of deception. If, however, we can learn from pain, it is not wasted but a source of life and health.

Four Decades of Weakness

Physicians note that microbes and germs are always around. Whether a person is healthy depends in part on his or her ability to fight off the microorganisms. In the same sense, anxious forces are ever present in organizations. The level of disease depends in part on the community's equivalent of the body's processes for warding off viruses: its vitality; its sense of morale, its members' commitment to share goals, its immune response.

If either organisms or organizations adapt to weakness, they encourage disease processes. The following story is about how a congregation and pastor became locked into emotional dependence with each other.

For thirty-three years, Pastor Miller laid his hand on the brittle soul of the congregation. They feared what he feared;

they drummed the beat he drummed. When he ridiculed new Bible translations, condemned contemporary music, and opposed gambling, the ranks of the faithful drew closer together. Sealed in a collective paranoia, the people focused their wrath on ungodly, external forces or people.

Nearly ten years after his departure, Pastor Miller's fingers were still fiddling with the soft soul of the congregation from his retirement home only a few miles away. Four successive pastors had left. His immediate successor stayed for two years after being accused of sexual malfeasance. (He was ultimately acquitted.) The next pastor survived thirty months, leaving because he was no longer willing to subject his family and himself to random and covert criticism. The fourth pastor stayed barely a year.

Miller's shadow loomed large in the psyche of this congregation. He was the "ghost emeritus"—not there, yet there. On the wall overlooking the fellowship hall was a photograph of Miller, framed in gold and illuminated by a light that was never turned off.

When the congregation's board voted twelve to three not to contract with me to help them discover why their pastors kept leaving, the bishop called to inform me of the decision. He said he was going to leave them alone. They were threatening to leave the denomination. I jested, "You should be so lucky." But I added, "You know what's happening, and you are doing nothing. You are now part of the system, part of the problem." A week later the bishop called to get my feedback on his proposal to deal with Pastor Miller. He planned to present to Miller and his wife the "bishop's boundaries" for both of them regarding their former congregation.

Adaptation to the weakness was broken—finally! Gradually Pastor Miller withdrew, agreeing to comply with most of the bishop's boundaries. The weakness was the persistent arrangement of dependency. Pastor Miller was weak in his capacity to differentiate. Little emotional space existed between the retired pastor and the parish he had served.

A House Divided against Itself

Emotional systems must face anxiety's uproar. Unfortunately, anxious reactivity intensifies conflict, builds resistance, and divides the house. Two highly anxious parties become automatic, defensive, and then caught in a spiral of opposition.

Organisms use opposing forces to maintain balance and to regulate life. Muscles, for example, are set in opposition: one contracts while its opposite relaxes. Organizations work well with checks and balances. They employ people at the opposite ends of issues: the "bottom line" people counterbalanced by the "sky's the limit" people. Opposition becomes negative when the forces tighten and reject the opposite. Instead of being a balancing force, opposition becomes a divisive one.

A three-page letter addressed to Kevin Perry, the key lay official at Memorial Church, outlined eight reasons why Rev. Barton Wells should be asked to resign:

1. We are not being spiritually fed.
2. We believe the pastor spends too much time with community activities to the neglect of members.
3. We feel the pastor cares for a select group of people only.
4. We think his top-down management style is inappropriate for this congregation, which has many skilled, talented people.
5. We know that other churches are growing. We are growing but not as rapidly. Why?
6. We believe Rev. Wells has been stifling Rev. Spears's ministry.
7. We believe the youth program needs more attention from the pastor, but he refused to heed our warning.
8. Rev. Wells isn't discrete about information given to him confidentially.

Attached to the letter was a page containing 26 signatures. Kevin brought the letter to the attention of the governing board. He shared a copy with both pastors. The board decided to invite the signers to a special meeting. They, in turn, accepted the invitation, though initially they refused because the board would not accept their condition that Rev. Wells not attend the meeting.

Nearly two-thirds of the people requesting Rev. Wells's resignation had opposed the two-year ministry of Blair Bridgen eight years ago. Some of the charges brought against Blair bore a resemblance to those against Rev. Wells. Nine months of hassling had followed after charges were made against Blair. Finally Blair relented, resigned, and removed himself from the church's clergy roster.

The bitterness that followed seeped into the capillaries of Memorial's blood system. For several years people would not talk to certain people. The two different worship services almost became camp grounds identifying each of the warring parties. In the last two years, however, the acrimonious atmosphere had given way to a new spirit. The letter, then, opened old wounds.

Kevin realized that if these people who had filed the complaint were not attended to, they would persist nonetheless. Yet he knew if they were catered to, their wounding of other members a second time might bring worse consequences. Kevin Perry's position as director of the board may have been divine intervention. He was not paralyzed in the face of differences and opposition. He did not think in terms of "good versus bad." What was happening at Memorial, therefore, would not devolve into black/white thinking. To Kevin, Memorial reminded him of families in perpetual crisis. They take sides, and they take hostages. But he would not let those involved split the difference, as had happened eight years ago. He was determined not to give in to the sulky, offended people. Likewise, he would not play protector of the hurt, defending party. The board was going to take a stand. The parties, Kevin believed, would have to learn to live with the outcome. He had the rare ability to see the whole, to see how the offenders and the defenders compose a system.

Memorial was fortunate to have Kevin's leadership. To be healthy requires taking an effective *stand* in the middle of those who are taking sides or hostages. Of course, the result may be partial peace. The people may enter a truce and be decent to one another, yet not really overcome the differences. The hard truth is that this is far from the best of all possible worlds. Some things lie beyond resolution.

For Reflection and Discussion

1. How is your congregation working with the core issues (page 43)? Describe goals and actions applicable to each issue.
2. Review the chart on clergy-focused and mission-focused congregations (pages 46–47). Note the ways your congregation is clergy focused. What actions could you take to move from being clergy-focused to being mission-focused?
3. Review the four cases studies (pages 48–56). What issues are common to the four congregations? What issues are unique to each congregation? What can you learn about your congregation from these case studies?

Chapter 5

Infectious Anxiety

All "reaction to" is very easily converted into "reaction against."

—*José Ortega y Gasset*

Anxious systems diagnose people instead of their relationships.

—*Edwin Friedman*

Almost anything is easier to get into . . . than out of.

—*Agnes Allen*

The outcome of our interactions with the environment depends just as much upon our reactions to the stressor as upon the nature of the stressor itself

—*Hans Selye*

Murmuring

"An element of sickness gets into the body," Dietrich Bonhoeffer writes in *Life Together*, "perhaps nobody knows where it comes from or in what member it has lodged, but the body is infected."[1] The apostle Paul made many references to infections in the early church: "grumblers, malcontents...loudmouthed boasters" (Jude 16 RSV), people who "bite and devour one another" (Galatians 5:15), groups unbending in their contentiousness (1 Corinthians 1:10-17). He warns against "godless chatter," "a man who is fractious," and "quarreling, jealousy, anger, selfishness, slander, gossip, conceit, and disorder." Further, he is forthright and personal, saying. "Alexander the coppersmith did me great harm" (2 Timothy 4:14). Obviously members of the early church had to contend with both quarrelsome opponents and their own hostile spirits.

In the Old Testament the same theme is evident in the Israelites' "murmurings against the Lord" (Exodus 16:7). Even the Lord says, "How long must I tolerate the complaints of this wicked community?" (Numbers 14:27 NEB). Moses gets caught in the crossfire. The people "raised an outcry" against him, complaining. "Why have you brought us out of Egypt with our children and our herds to let us all die of thirst?" (Exodus 17:7 NEB). It all started when the people of God, nostalgic for their Egyptian diet spiced by garlic and sweetened by melon, became hungry. God sent manna. They gathered it up excitedly, were content and grateful. But soon they were displeased once again. As people do when times get hard, they expressed their bitterness: "We loathe this worthless food" (Numbers 21:5 RSV).

Two New Testament writers, Luke and John, use the Greek verb *goggizo* (to grumble, murmur, speak complainingly against someone, speak secretly or in whisper) on several occasions:

And the Pharisees and the Scribes murmured, saying, "This man receives sinners and eats with them" (Luke 15:2 RSV).

Now in these days when the disciples were increasing in number, the Hellenists murmured against the Hebrews because their widows were neglected in the daily distribution (Acts 6:1).

The Jews then murmured at him, because he said "I am the bread which came down from heaven" (John 6:41).

But Jesus, knowing in himself that his disciples murmured at it, said to them, "Do you take offense at this?" (John 6:61).

The Israelites, the Hellenists, the Pharisees, the disciples, and Alexander prefigure the murmurers in the contemporary church. Grumbling is apparently endemic to human beings and, among some, epidemic. Put people together and inevitably someone will express contrariness.

Viral Infection

In a human community, murmurers *function* much in the same ways as viruses in a human body. Similarities exist between viral infection and relational conflict. A host cell (person, group) tolerates the virus's invasive behavior. It offers the virus free room and board.

The single purpose of a virus is to replicate itself. It is an intracellular parasite. It invades cells of other organisms. Outside living cells, a virus is incapable of multiplying. Once a virus gains entrance into a cell, it takes over the inner working of the host cell, draws out the nutrients, and then runs off copies of itself.

Characteristics of a virus include:

- cannot say "no" to itself
- has no boundary, respects no boundary
- cannot regulate itself, goes where it doesn't belong
- has no ability to learn from its experience
- cannot sacrifice for the sake of other cells
- is an intracellular parasite with no life of its own

Viruses abound in the human body, but few pose threat. They are very selective about the types and conditions of the cells they infect. Viruses are activated only in the cells they affect. The infection depends upon the interaction between the surface of the virus and the host cell. Sometimes a virus will hide its proteins from the immune system by altering its surface. It tricks the defense system. Consequently the memory cells cannot detect it. Resorting to subterfuge, a virus gets what it wants, and a host cell cooperates. Viral infection results from the destruction of the invaded cells or the impairment of the activities of the cells they invade. The host cell provides the virus with shelter and nourishment. Our bodies are their home and dinner. Complete damage benefits neither the virus nor the host cell. The survival of the parasitical virus depends on the host's continual survival and ability to provide resources for it.

The host cell's functioning influences the outcome of an infection. To illustrate, an acute measles infection makes an immense demand on the body's supply of vitamin A. Many Third World children are deficient in vitamin A. If infected with measles, these children are depleted of vitamin A. Many children die as a result of the host cell's cooperation with the measles virus.

Take the virus we call cancer. It loses its ability to stop growing. Cancer cells keep growing and multiplying. In essence, cancer cells say to the rest of the body, "I have no need of you. I exist for my own sake. You feed me." They grow and multiply. Cancer cells, grown wild, no longer act in regard for the rest of the body. Malignant, they spread rapidly throughout the body, choking out normal cells. Cancer cells are antisocial, just not caring what happens as long as they survive.

The Anxiety Virus

What can we learn from viral infections that will assist us in dealing with their counterpart, murmuring, in a congregation? What generally happens when a virus enters the body of Christ, threatening to infect it? In relationships, if murmuring is encouraged (finds a host cell), there will be infection. Anxiety flares up. Reactive behaviors take hold. In fact, reaction on the cellular level within an organism closely reflects reactive functioning between anxious people and groups.

Similar to a virus, anxiety needs a host cell in order to replicate itself. All forms of murmuring require the reinforcement of a host cell (cells) to continue and to grow. Four viruses are potentially virulent and can turn a congregation into a virtual "hot zone"—an anxiety pit. The viruses are *secrets* (gossiping, whispering), *accusations* (blaming, faultfinding), *lies* (deceiving), and *triangulation* (shifting burdens elsewhere). They are all expressions of the virus of anxiety. The presence of secrets or triangles are not themselves the disease. Rather, secrets and triangles enable the disease process. The disease requires a combination of the secrecy and the host cells (people who permit secrets to exist).

Murmuring Underground

One of the meanings of the Greek word *goggizo* is to speak secretly or in a whisper. Nothing is more difficult to confront than hidden complaints. What is unknown and concealed cannot be healed. The Danish philosopher Søren Kierkegaard said that in order for the wound to be healed, the wound must be kept open. In a similar comment, Supreme Court judge Louis Brandeis remarked that sunlight is the best disinfectant.

Speaking in Cleveland to a group of Episcopal clergy, I became aware of how secrecy is associated with the survival mentality. A priest revealed that he was legally blind and had a pet turtle. One day he was playing with the turtle when the phone rang in another room. He set the pet on the floor and went into that other room to answer the phone. He stayed on the phone longer than he had anticipated and hesitated to return to the room where his turtle was. He was afraid of stepping on it. When his wife returned home, he told her his dilemma. She laughed and said, "Bob, knowing the brain of that turtle, you know where you'll find him—in some dark corner." That is exactly where they found the turtle. When we are anxious, we make much use of the reptile brain. We are imprecise, vague, covert, less transparent. We operate in darkness. Secrecy is a deadly virus. Undetected, it can do untold damage, lasting for years. How can a congregation be a healthy community if it lives in darkness, keeps skeletons in the closet, and allows destructive disease processes to continue?

Secrets are infectious. They maintain other pathological forces. Secrets produce triangles. A tells B about C. A and B know; C does not know. C is placed in the outside position, where it is easier for A and B to depersonalize C, even more to distance emotionally from C. They can pin or bind their anxiety on C. Secrecy is an anxious reaction to anxiety.

If A and B are anxious, who else will become their target? Who else will be placed in position C? Further, if A and B are anxious, they may well orchestrate cryptic gatherings. They go off to some dark corner. Secret meetings are not arranged for the welfare of the whole community, nor are they dialogical in nature. Secret meetings achieve one thing. They place someone in the C position, someone we call a "scapegoat" or "identified patient." Someone is isolated to catch the anxiety of A and B (and possibly others). Secret meetings are divisive. One group knows; the others do not. The tone of secret gatherings is always serious. If the participants emerge as self-appointed vigilantes, another disease is in the making.

It is the secrecy of such meetings, not their content, that is the chief concern. Secret behavior is reactive behavior. It is utterly neglectful of the evangelical counsel "to speak the truth in love." In the New Testament three prominent situations address anxious reactivity in the Christian community: the Matthean sayings (Matthew 5:21-24; 7:3; 18:15-22); the Council of Jerusalem (Acts 15); and the chaos at Corinth (1 Corinthians 1:12; 3:4). Each situation calls for personalizing the conflict, face-to-face meetings, and sunlight for disinfecting the disease.

Secrets support immaturity. Underground murmurers in a community are usually insecure, dependent, and childish people. Whenever leaders protect their immature behaviors through silence, they enable it. If the leaders of a congregation refuse to address clandestine activity, they express their own anxiety. Ineffective leadership and gossipers, whisperers, and hidden complainers go together. They tie up the system in anxious knots. They promote disease processes.

You, You, You

Feeling dissatisfied or uneasy is not pathological. Pathology emerges when the dissatisfaction or uneasiness ripens into bitter accusation against others. "You didn't save me." "You haven't fixed me." "You don't care about us." "You are a disappointment to us." The accuser places responsibility for his or her own dissatisfaction on another. People use others to relieve themselves of their own pain. A faulted person gets pinned with the pain: "*You* are the reason I am unhappy." Immature people believe that the answer to their displeasure is simple: "*You* must do something; *you* must change."

Accusation is a virus. It is capable of draining life out of living cells. But as an expression of anxiety, it still needs another cell's reactivity to maintain itself. It needs "feedback"—food in return, nutrients from another cell. Sometimes the food comes in the form of countercharges. Sometimes accusations are reinforced by the accused defending, explaining, or justifying herself or himself. Critical, hostile people cannot create infection alone. Host cells always contribute to viral infection by providing nutrients.

Critical judgment does not change anyone or anything in the universe. If you dislike someone or react negatively toward a certain behavior, it does not change the person or the behavior you are judging. When you judge another critically, you do not define that person. You define yourself. Your harsh judgment says something about you. It describes your likes and dislikes. Accusation—"you, you, you"—is really about "me."

The People of the Lie

Deceit is the hallmark of evil. At times evil plays its hand in congregational life and, sadly, may even be encouraged. Priest

and author Richard John Neuhaus warns against "the danger
of giving evil dynamics a kind of legitimacy in the life of the
Church." He explicitly argues that "some evils are not to be
worked out and some conflicts are not to be managed—they
are simply not to be admitted into the community's life at all."
Short of reconciliation and repentance, Neuhaus urges that there
be restraint of evil forces.

Deceit is cover up, falsity, and darkness. The evil avoid
anything that sheds light, anything that involves exposure. The
evil, M. Scott Peck remarks, are "the people of the lie." Where
there is evil, there is a lie present. The evil are not truthful. It
is the nature of evil to find a disguise. No wonder, then, Peck
claims that "evil people tend to gravitate toward piety" and "one
of the places evil people are most likely to be found is within
the church."[2]

We can recognize "the people of the lie" in several ways.
The evil are self-absorbed. Never giving a second thought, they
sacrifice others for their own purposes. In the presence of evil,
you feel a sense of revulsion. You do not like being near these
people. You recoil from their presence. You may also experience
confusion. Something does not logically fit; something is not
complete. Moreover, the evil are adept at scapegoating, placing
blame "out there." So often they appear to be on the side of
righteousness. They are known too by their willfulness. They
are stubborn and perverse, determined to have their own way.

The manifestation of evil I encounter most frequently in
the church is the cunning, sly kind—subtle manipulation,
winsome seductiveness, shrewd innocence. In fact, I dare to
say that the cunning side of evil is even assisted, enabled, and
welcomed in the church. It is as if the environment of the
congregation itself encourages and cooperates with this type of
virus.

The wife of a pastor who sexually seduced a half dozen
women in his parish told me she could predict who would be

her husband's next target. "I could see it in his eyes, the way he looked at her," she commented. "You know, the 'evil eye' thing." She looked at me directly, saying, "He would tell them that sex with him was like having the Lord's Supper. Can you believe that?" Turning her face away, she became quiet. Then she spoke again: "How could they have been so stupid?" Once again she looked at me and spoke tearfully:

> I believed his nonsense...just like his victims. It was two parts Jesus, one part charm, one part sweet talk, a half cup of syrup...who cares....Distortion, all of it. I thought submission meant going brain dead....Slippery, real slippery. But he was a master, a fantastic deceiver.

Before she left my office, she asked several piercing questions: Why are people so eager to be mystified? Why does it seem easier to get fooled, suckered in, or enchanted in the church than elsewhere? Why is there such gullibility? Why are people who are fraudulent and self-serving mistaken for being spiritual and committed?

I had a couple of lengthy luncheon conversations with a former chief executive officer of a large company. Retired, he now spent a chunk of his time at his church. "There's too much fuzziness," he mentioned, "like who is accountable to whom." He contrasted his experience in business with his recent activity at the parish. "I don't like the indefiniteness. The blurring and haziness that is allowed," he lamented. "Why, it increases temptation and possibly chicanery." As he talked about his experience, I thought to myself that he was describing a system problem. Why does the virus of deceit find opportunity in host cells in the church? Why are people in the church such easy prey for the sneaky? We seem utterly prone to be taken in by wolves in sheep's clothing. Peck mentions the disguise offered by piety. But I think there is another side to the coin: Congregations are far too willing to accommodate the clever deceptions of "the people of the lie." We need to balance being "innocent as doves" with being "wise as serpents."

Triangulation

Remember the children's rhyme, "Green Grow the Rushes-O." It begins, "One is one and all alone and ever more shall be so." Indeed we live alone. Inevitably, though, we long for another: "Two, two are the lily white boys, a-clothed all in green-o." It is the nature of relationships to proceed eventually to: "Three, three are the rivals." Conflict, rivalry, relationship tension. Three is the key number.

In periods of conflict, a third party's presence is logical—and emotional. It is logical because the ones who are less able to settle a dispute are the disputants themselves. A constructive approach is to usher in a mediator to arbitrate the impasse between two factions.

A third party's presence is also emotional. When conflict swells, triangles take shape. A two-person relationship is unstable when tension and anxiety exceed tolerable levels. Let's say Dick and Jane are anxious with each other. Dick, to relieve himself of his anxiety, says to Jane, "You are just as angry as your father." Dick puts himself in the outside position. Jane and her father are in the inside position. A third party is brought in to stabilize the situation between Dick and Jane.

"When elephants fight," a Swahili proverb states, "it's the grass that gets crushed." Triangulation is a natural way of handling anxiety. If anxiety in one relationship is not resolved, it will be played out in another relationship. A person feels relief from tension when anxiety is shifted to a third party, yet the anxiety in the original relationship is unchanged. It has been merely relocated.

You know a triangle exists when you experience the following:

- The reactivity being expressed toward you is excessive, strong, and far beyond what might be normal.
- Someone is overfocused on you.
- You look for a sympathetic third person who will share your irritation with an adversary.
- You turn to a second party to talk about a third party.
- You become allied with a friend against your friend's opponent.
- You need to rescue, care for your friend when he or she is anxious.
- You pin your anxiety on someone to relieve tension that belongs to another relationship.

Anyone who grew up in the human family will find triangle formation natural. Many triangles are not destructive. They are transient and passing. "When triangles become intense, rigid, and indissoluble," professor David Augsburger states, "all the relationships involved tend to deteriorate."[3] People react to one another more and respond less. Perception is incredibly distorted. Instead of working on problems, people blame one another.

Certainly all kinds of viruses could infect a congregation. I have noted four prominent ones. Actually the identity of the particular virus is secondary. What is primary is whether or not the viruses are encouraged. Albeit Schweitzer once said that serious illness did not bother him for long because he was too inhospitable a host. Anxious, reactive people never victimize automatically. Like a virus, they insist that you adapt to them. Nevertheless the key variable is always your own response.

Brain-Based Behavior

"Every act of self-control of the Christian is also a service to the fellowship," Lutheran theologian Dietrich Bonhoeffer notes. "Every member serves the whole body, either to its health or to its destruction."[4] If you *initiate* the murmuring or *enable* it, you contribute to the destructive side. The antidote to both kinds of reactive behaviors is self-control. How, then, do we move from being reactive to being responsive? To understand our behavior, we need to examine the functioning of the human brain.

"I still find it difficult," neurologist Richard Restak exclaims, "to believe that this three-pound mass of protoplasm with the consistency of an overripe avocado is the seat of who I am, of who we all are."[5] The three-pound mass of protoplasm, the human brain, is arranged in three tiers. Each of the three brains is to some extent independent, having its own special function. The three brains function as three legislative branches competing for "executive power." From top to bottom (and from larger to smaller), there is the thinking brain, the feeling brain, and the reactive brain.

If a person's neo-cortex (thinking brain) were removed, we basically would have eliminated that person's identity, or humanity. Beneath the cortex is the limbic system (feeling brain), not much different from the brain of a Bengal tiger, Scottish terrier, or Arctic fox. Below the limbic system is the R-system (reptile or reactive brain). It approximates that of a rattlesnake or salamander.

When stress and anxiety are high, the R-system is exaggerated. In other words, people become more thoughtless, more instinctive, and more automatic. The same is true concerning the feeling brain. Once fueled by limbic-derived feelings, we have less access to the thinking brain. Both brains have ensured the survival of the individual and the species. Necessary to survival, feelings have an insistent quality and are hardwired into the nervous system. With strong arousal, the limbic brain can be driven to continue. The reactive force can go on for hours. Highly excited emotional states are like poison ivy—we become all itch.

One of the functions of the thinking brain is to exercise veto power over the instinctive forces of the two lower brains. It sets

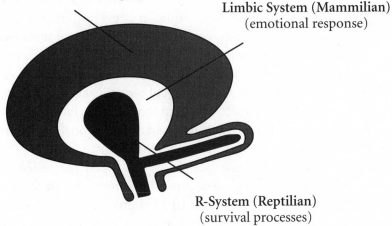

Neo-Cortex
(conscious rational thought)

Limbic System (Mammilian)
(emotional response)

R-System (Reptilian)
(survival processes)

Neo-Cortex (Thinking)	**Limbic System (Feeling)**	**R-System (Reacting)**
• attention • mental problem solving • many choices • organizing world • memory • thought-out behavior • source of values, beliefs, convictions • "light" shedding	• connection • regulating stable environment (blood pressure, temperature, sugar level, immune system) • very few choices • bonding with others • play • emotional behavior • source of community • "warm" giving	• automation • sensory motor, physical processes (approach-avoid, fight-flight) • no choices • preserving self • safety • survival behavior • source of reactivity • "cold" acting

limits on behavior; it provides self-control. This is one reason
moral codes are stated in the negative—"Thou shalt not…"
Nonetheless the lower brains, more automatic and defensive
than the thinking brain, have a quicker triggering effect and do
not easily defer to the thinking brain. We can fool ourselves,
thinking that we are using the neo-cortex when in reality we are
being driven by the limbic system. A common example of this
situation is the defense mechanism of rationalization. When we
rationalize, we use the neo-cortex in service of the limbic system.
Rationalization is more automatic than intentional. It is more
concerned about survival than enlightenment.

Neurologist Richard Restak has discussed the difference
between limbic "firing" and cortical "monitoring" in the case
of Bernard Goetz, the individual who fired at his assailants in
a New York city subway a decade ago. Goetz was brought to
trial. The prosecuting attorney did not contest Goetz's cause
for apprehension. He argued that Goetz, once aroused, should
have been able to stop himself. One of his attackers was shot,
helpless, and unable to harm Goetz further. Yet Goetz fired a
second shot at him. The attorney contended that Goetz did not
act in a rational, responsible manner; the attorney reasoned that
Goetz, once out of "harm's way," should have "cooled" the situation. Restak argues, however, that such thinking is outmoded.
It emphasizes the power of the thinking brain to prevail. But
Restak says that these expectations are sometimes neurologically

Human Brain

RAY JOHNSON

unrealistic. Once provoked to a furious state of self-preservation, the feeling brain can issue directive force for hours, being resistant to an immediate switch to cortical thinking.[6]

For Reflection and Discussion

1. Review the characteristics of a virus (pages 59–60). What signs do you see that a virus is at work in your congregation?
2. Four viruses are described on page 61. Review the case studies in chapter 4 (pages 48–56). Which viruses are at work in each congregation?
3. Identify present or past situations in your congregation that provide evidence of one or more viruses at work. How has the congregation responded to those viruses? What has the presence of the viruses meant for the health of your congregation?
4. When anxiety becomes infectious, any of the following might be true of a system:

   Polarization, rigid opposition, all-or-nothing thinking
   Serious tone, tense mood
   Scapegoating, blaming, criticizing
   Yearning for quick fixes, impatience
   Withdrawal, cut-offs, distancing
   Crisis orientation
   Indecisiveness
   Unbelievably selfish behavior
   Diagnosis of others
   Looking for clear causes
   Black-and-white, either/or thinking
   Group think, being stuck together
   Lack of curiosity
   Magical thinking (everything will be all right)
   Leaders don't take stands
   Increases in attacks, sense of urgency

Vague, nebulous complaints
Loss of broad perspective
Magnification of difference
Unwillingness to learn

Circle the characteristics present in your congregation. How can these be dealt with?

Chapter 6

The Coconut Captivity of the Church

*The only unsafe group is a closed one, a world in which
awareness of change is not present.*

—Arnold Mindell

*Just as individuals resist the pain and dislocation that comes
with changing their attitudes and habits of behavior, societies
resist learning as well.*

—Ronald Heifetz

*We must always change, renew, regenerate ourselves; otherwise
we harden.*

—Johann von Goethe

*This is a world of permanent white water in which we're all
roaring down a wild river, none of us feeling like we either
understand or control what we're in the middle of.*

—Peter Vaill

Rigidity

In *Zen and the Art of Motorcycle Maintenance*, Robert Pirsig
describes how monkeys are captured in India. A coconut shell
is hollowed out and chained to a stake. The shell is filled with
rice. An aperture is carved out, just wide enough for a monkey's
hand to go through but too narrow for a fist filled with rice to
exit. The monkey is trapped by its own rigidity. As Pirsig notes,
the monkey cannot understand that "freedom without rice is
more valuable than capture with it."[1]

All living forms are endangered when they lack flexibility. Someone has said that disease is the organism's failure to adapt. Despite significant fluctuations in environmental conditions, a healthy organism regulates levels of sugar, salt, and fluids. It knows how to maintain stability in the face of ongoing, external change. To live well, an organism must adapt to the changes of the environment in which it lives.

Rigidity, therefore, could be hazardous to an organization's health. When a congregation is trapped by its own resistance to change, the congregation resembles the monkey. The congregation cannot understand that openness to change is more valuable than fear of it.

The Tomato Effect

Even if evidence stares us in the face that something is needed or effective, we may reject it. If it does not fit our ideas or if we do not want to change course, we can deny, neglect, or trivialize the evidence. Information always has an emotional side to it. The phenomenon has been called the "tomato effect."

The tomato was discovered by Europeans in the New World. Explorers brought it to Spain and from there it spread quickly to Italy and France. The Italians called it "pomodoro"; the French ascribed aphrodisiac properties to the tomato, "pomme d'amour." By the end of the sixteenth century, the tomato had become a regular ingredient in European meals.[2]

Strangely, the South American fruit transformed European cuisine but had minimal acceptance in North America. Belonging to the nightshade family of plants, some of which are poisonous, the tomato was not grown in North America. Cultivating tomatoes was cultivating death. Despite the fact the Italians and French were harvesting and ingesting tomatoes in larger and larger quantities, the belief persisted that tomatoes induced death.

Harvard business professor Theodore Levitt wrote a classic article on the "tomato effect." He focused on the demise of the railroad industry in America. At the turn of the century, railroads did not cease growing because people and freight no longer needed transportation. According to Levitt, the railroads declined because they believed they were in the railroad business, not the transportation business. Alternative means of transportation developed. The railroads stayed mired in their narrow view. They confused means (railroad) with ends (transportation).[3]

In contrast to the story of the railroads is the genius of the Stanley Tool Company. They train their salespeople not to sell electric drills but to sell "holes." (It is believed that laser drills will soon replace electric ones). Stanley is in the "hole" business. They keep a purpose, a goal, or an end in view. The means are simply ways to get there, not the ends themselves.

How many congregations believe they are in the "we exist for ourselves" business rather than the "we are in mission to the community, even the world" business? How many congregations confuse "the way we have done things for decades" with the "larger apostolic purposes"? How many congregations mistake the means for the ends?

Howling at Hosanna

Hosanna is a congregation that has prided itself for years on its excellent music program. People come from significant distances to attend worship services at Hosanna. The music has been largely traditional, supported by many choirs and different instrumentation. The music program spans all age groups.

Two years ago the congregation hired a church consultant to help the leadership give direction to the future. Half of Hosanna's 1,400 members are over fifty years of age. As age creep continues, fewer and fewer individuals will travel the distance from their homes to Hosanna. Other changes will happen. For example, there will be an increased need for home visitation of the elderly. One of the consultant's recommendations was to develop and introduce an alternate form of worship. Surrounding Hosanna are numerous apartments with young adults and neighborhoods with older, smaller homes. Young families are starting to move into the neighborhoods because of the affordability of the houses. Some of Hosanna's leaders believe the congregation needs to turn its attention to the immediate vicinity. Others propose that the congregation does not need to change its style of music or worship to accommodate potential members.

The leaders favoring the addition of an alternative worship service suggested that it be held on Saturday evening, possibly Sunday night. The two Sunday morning services, which average 390 and 340 respectively, would not be changed.

Public discussions were held. Many viewpoints were expressed with civility and fair-mindedness. What completely surprised many leaders was "the petition." It appeared a week after the public meeting. Carrying the names of seventy-eight people, it had importance. But why, many leaders puzzled, hadn't these people come forward at the open forum? Basically, the petition requested that no new worship service be initiated. On the one hand, the leaders were commended for their openness, but on the other hand, they were condemned for "the fear of diminishment." God, the petition stated, would provide the means of survival and growth. Also, the church consultant used in the planning process was cited as an "unsuccessful parish pastor," therefore questionable as an adequate resource.

The leaders retreated. If they advanced their plans, they feared reprisals. Maybe, they reasoned, if they waited for a while, the steep opposition would be lowered. To an outsider, the leaders appeared to capitulate to the opposition forces too early. After all, reactive and resistant forces to the "new" are as natural in organizations as in organisms. Still, the situation proves how powerful emotional forces can be, creating an almost unbreakable "stuck togetherness."

Thinking systemically, we realize that a change in one part affects other parts and other systems. Change is never singular in its effect. Moreover, the brain involved in matters of survival fires quickly and imprecisely. Reactivity serves the forces of resistance and may occur at any step in a planned change process, even after public, open forums. Sufficiently threatened, we are at the mercy of impulse. Self-preservation is imprinted in our nerves. Once the automatic brain is aroused, our behaviors are more rigid, defensive, and mindless. We hold onto the rice with a tighter fist. We sign petitions or cater to them.

The Shock of the New

No generation has had to face greater and more prolonged change than the present one. Thirty years after Alvin Toffler's *Future Shock*, we are living it. Toffler equated future shock with "the shattering stress and disorientation that we induce in individuals by subjecting them to too much change in too short a time." When anyone's "absorption capacity" is exceeded, the person displays symptoms from irritation to blame, from reduced trust to a victim mentality, from psychic numbing to a search for messiahs. There are simply limits to the ability to absorb all the change that is happening.[4]

During the 1994 Rwandan refugee work, a relief worker reported to her supervisors that working in that area was like working in an open graveyard and sewer. She pleaded with them not to dispatch relief workers for more than a few weeks at a time. The workers, selected as much for their emotional resilience as professional skill, found that their psychological energy was greatly exhausted considering the conditions. Skilled relief workers, called to deal with grotesque calamities, were asked to work beyond their "absorption capacities." The shock of the new diminished the most emotionally hardy person. Knowing their assignment would be brief, however, gave volunteers the energy needed to cope with the chaos and horror. Returning from their short-term stints, relief workers could seek help for themselves through psychological counseling.

The Old English word "wyrd" and the English word "weird" have their source in the German word "werden," meaning "to become." Whenever there is a period of becoming or change, there is weirdness. We now appear to be going through a transitional period. Something is on the way out, and something else is painfully coming to life. Family therapist Edwin Friedman believes we are in a period of "societal regression," a period of heightened reactivity and lessened responsibility for self. Behaviorally, this means we are putting more energy into the automatic brain, the survival brain. It is designed to be instinctive and defensive—and fast. There is no thought in this part of the brain. The lower brain permits no variation in an organism's response to a specific stimulus. The lower brain is a slave to the past; it has no sense of time; it is poor at handling new situations. Whatever is "registered" in its memory as a threat provokes, upon recurrence, a defensive behavior. The brain reacts to the present as if it were the past. It simply jumps to conclusions. Survival behaviors follow—fight, flight, freeze.

On Not Throwing Marshmallows

A Florida guide speaking to tourists warned them not to throw marshmallows and white bread to the alligators. He explained that the alligator's brain is "comparable to a baloney sandwich." Reptiles do not have the mental capacity to distinguish one item from another. They have no differentiating mechanism. Hence the marshmallow and your hand—and your arm and the rest of you—are all one of a piece to an alligator.

In our topsy-turvy world, the reptile brain is poised for quick release. When it senses great danger, it will even take over the control center from the other brains. That is the same thing as saying that terrorism, militia groups, and fanaticism are increasing. Sufficiently threatened, we are at the mercy of impulse. Self-preservation is imprinted in our nerves. When intensely anxious, we react and lash out or pull back. We have less capacity to *differentiate*. If someone returns our anxiety with their own, it's a marshmallow war.

The more energy we direct to the survival brain, the less energy is available for the thinking brain, which allows us to be more resilient, imaginative, and reflective. Without the thinking brain's ability to self-regulate automatic processes, adaptation is impossible. Little energy is available for novelty, probing alternatives, and increasing options. When the lower brain dominates, things are cut and dried, unbending, and never surprising. Daniel Coleman, science writer for *The New York Times*, illustrates:

> Much evidence testifies that people who are emotionally adept—who know and manage their own feelings well, and who read and deal effectively with other people's feelings—are at an advantage in any domain of life, whether romance and intimate relationships or picking up the unspoken rules that govern success in organizational politics. People with well-developed emotional skills are also more likely to be content and effective in their lives, mastering the habits of mind that foster their own productivity; people who cannot marshal some control over their emotional life fight inner battles that sabotage their ability for focused work and clear thought.[5]

Family therapist Murray Bowen said something to the same effect when he said that people who are chronically anxious are driven more by their own emotional forces. They suffer more and take longer to recover. Obviously rigidity, stiffness, and taut tension are hazardous to an individual's life—and to a congregation. We become captive to old, defensive behaviors.

Captive Hearts

A special "captivity"—one that is incredibly hard to break free of—is what I call the "romance." The pastor and the congregation "fall in love." Systems theory calls it being emotionally "stuck together." It happens with long pastorates of twenty to thirty years. It can just as easily happen in short pastorates of four to six years, especially if the pastor developed the congregation.

Romance is blindness to reality. It is illusion. Romantics idealize one another. Being myopic, they are selective about what they are aware of and remember. Faults and deficits are largely invisible. Romance is being under an anesthetic or a spell.

When pastor and congregation fall in love, they have a "tie that blinds." The pastor is regarded as "one of a kind." Compared to other clergy, Rev. Special is far superior. In return, the adoring congregation is rewarded with "good feelings" and a specialness of its own.

Usually the pastor is charming, ambitious, outwardly confident, always cheerful, and positive. Quite often the pastor excels as a crisis counselor or as a "rainmaker," bringing in people and money. Very few pastors in these situations care about the rigors of thinking. They want to touch the heart. As a rule, the pastor's sermons are anecdotal, folksy, upbeat, and motivational. The people are enchanted. It's as if the Sunday worship service provides a narcotic or fix. More appropriate to romance, worship is an aphrodisiac.

Both parties have an attachment problem. Clergy and congregation are too emotionally entwined. Without sufficient distance, they cannot see each other clearly. Their romance, though, is a spurious wholeness. The two sides project positively onto one another. Thus the one cannot change or disappoint the other because that would alter the relationship arrangement. To maintain the romantic glow, each party plays its role. This is the deal: you soothe and stroke me, I'll soothe and stroke you. When people become overinvested and fixated on one another, they are emotionally fused. In *Intimate Worlds*, Maggie Scarf depicts a fused family in which one family member says, "When one of us has a headache, we all take an aspirin."[6]

Realistically, many pastor-congregation relationships are romantic. When a pastor first arrives, the period is called the "honeymoon." If it goes on and on, the romance has started. Two parties dissolve into one. Any movement toward differentiation is considered treasonous. If, however, one of the parties fails to match the partner's ideal, what was once "kisses and roses" turns into "scowls and lemons." Or if one of the partners gains awareness, breaking through the romantic spell, that party will function in new ways. The second party becomes upset, does everything possible to return the relationship to the former pattern, and short of that, turns against the other. Blackmail tactics replace honeymoon tactics. Either way, the two parties are emotionally stuck together.

Of course, the opposite type of relationship can develop, too. Pastor and congregation never connect. Either the pastor leaves in one or two years or the congregation sees to it that it happens. Instead of romance, the two parties fear getting too close. This is also an emotional arrangement. Like romance, the alienation is a rigid pattern of functioning. Both parties create enemies.

Many years ago, theologian Richard Niebuhr declared that the purpose of the ministry and the congregation is "the increase of the love of God and neighbor." By love, Niebuhr meant an attitude of gratitude and respect: "Love is reverence; it keeps its distance even as it draws near; it does not seek to absorb the other in the self or want to be absorbed by it."[7] This is a stark contrast to a romantic relationship or an alienated one between pastor and congregation.

Learning Points

Business consultant Peter Senge believes the organizations that will survive will be learning organizations.[8] Continuous learning keeps them flexible and adaptive. They create their future. Unfortunately rigid congregations do not learn. Blind to their own blindness, they fail to see what they are embedded in. Rigid behaviors or patterns mean there is less awareness, less thinking, less self-control available.

Attesting to the creative aspect of unpredictable reality, Martin Luther observed, "Man never flies so high as when he knows not whither he is going." Our lives are full of stimuli to which we have no ready, adaptive response but in the face of which we must respond. Learning is struggling. But precisely because of the tension, we learn. To avert the struggle is to doom the learning. Disease is the body's way of saying that we have failed to adapt, adjust, or change to meet the situation, or that we have done so at the price of physical or mental disturbance.

For Reflection and Discussion

1. What evidence do you see that your congregation is or is not rigid (pages 73–74)? Who is involved?
2. What steps might have been taken to avert or diminish the "howling at Hosanna" (pages 75–77)?
3. What events in your congregation suggest the presence of a "romance" (pages 79–81)? Who is involved?
4. What do you think your congregation needs to learn (pages 81–82)? Why? What would this learning do for the life and mission of the congregation?

PART 3

HEALTH RESOURCES

Chapter 7

The Higher Medicines

Your faith has made you well.

          —Mark 5:34

So much of the creativity of a culture is a response to the reality of sickness.

          —Lawrence Sullivan

A high degree of imagination is required of those who trust in God.

          —Douglas John Hall

Real community is not homogeneity. It is the discipline and devotion of disparate people bearing with one another—the hard tasks of love.

          —Richard John Neuhaus

Response

It has been said that health comes from empowering people to take responsibility for their own health. The health of a congregation is no different. It comes from individuals being responsible, being stewards of the whole. Healthy people create healthy congregations. The congregation's health and the people in it are connected.

We have learned much from medical research in recent years about health as a response. For one thing, we know that the way a person responds to stressors is as important as the stressor itself. We know that beliefs, emotions, and meanings influence our immune responses. We know that human companionship is the best health insurance in the world. Mind-body research has illuminated how psychological states and relationship patterns play a prominent role in health outcome. Mood, anger, social support, loneliness, hopelessness, and purpose affect biochemical responses in the body. No wonder, then, helplessness is considered to be a disease in itself. The spirit is bruised or nauseated, and the energy necessary to respond adequately is not available. Of course, the opposite is true. As we say, "Good cheer is half the battle." Always, the response of the organism (organization) influences health.

What unique resources are available to healthy congregations? What type of responses strengthen the well-being of the body of Christ? What higher medicines bolster the healing process in a congregation?

Body and Soul

Martin Luther suffered numerous bodily ailments. He often associated the power of grace with physical relief or comfort. "For when the soul is healed," the reformer remarked, "the body has benefited also." He admitted to severe bouts with depression as well. Luther warned young people to shun loneliness because it could possibly lead to melancholy. Associating mind with body, he said: "Heavy thoughts bring on physical maladies. When the soul is oppressed so is the body." With a broad sweep, Luther said that the grace of God helps people in *all* their afflictions—body, mind, and spirit.

Luther easily found soul mates in the writers of the psalms and the apostle Paul, all of whom openly confronted their own human maladies and sought divine help. "There must, then, be a higher remedy, to wit, faith and prayer," Luther proposed, "just as Psalm 31:5 says, 'My times are in thy hand!'" (Incidentally, Luther suffered many physical ailments. If Paul had a "thorn in his flesh," Luther had the whole briar patch. One of Luther's bodily disturbances was constipation. Considering that the medicinal antidote administered to him was dung and garlic, it is no surprise that he searched for a "higher remedy.")

The higher medicines of faith and prayer are responses to life situations; they are *responses* to God. Certainly faith and prayer are not cure-alls. Rather, they are strengths for coping with and changing reality.

Faith and prayer are closely connected to Jesus's ministry of healing. After the crowds came to hear him and he healed them, it is said that "he went out to the mountain to pray; and he spent the night in prayer to God" (Luke 6:12). Standing before the tomb of Lazarus and before he cried out, "Come forth!" Jesus lifted his eyes upward and said, "Father, I thank thee that thou hast heard me" (John 11:41 RSV). On three occasions, Jesus said to the sick, "Your faith has made you well" (Mark 5:34; 10:57; Luke 17:15). To the blind man, Jesus said, "Do you believe that I am able to do this?" (Matthew 9:28). To the Canaanite woman, he exclaimed, "Woman, great is your faith! Let it be done for you as you wish," and her daughter was healed instantly (Matthew 15:28). When a paralyzed man lying on a bed was brought to Jesus, Jesus healed the man, noticing the faith of the people who carried his bed (Mark 2:1-12). Indeed, prayer and faith are higher remedies.

For Luther, the highest remedy is God's grace. He calls baptism "a priceless medicine" and the Lord's Supper "a soothing medicine." They are God's gifts, summoning our response of faith in the Giver and our love for others. Our response of faith and compassion is one relationship in two dimensions. Our relationship to God is connected to our relationship to other people. To be sons and daughters of the Father, we are brothers and sisters to the other sons and daughters. "As you have done it to one of the least of these my brethren, you have done it to me" (Matthew 25:40 RSV). God, others, and I constitute a system. We form a whole.

Being With

"When God wants to speak and deal with us," Luther said, "he does not avail himself of an angel but of parents, of the pastor, or of my neighbor." God wants to deal with us on the basis of the personal. Love is the primary means God has of using us to reveal himself in another. The "mutual conversation and consolation" of people is health promoting. St. John Chrysostom vividly depicted love as "the sacrament of the brother."

We are created for relationship. Creation is relational. The biblical record is replete with stories of the relationships between fathers and sons, mothers and children, husbands and wives, leaders and followers. The truth comes through the relational. Reality is known only in connections and interactions. And nothing conveys the relational better than the story. As Luther said, "The Gospel is nothing but the story of God's little son, and of his humbling."[1]

So many of the primary biblical concepts refer not to an entity or a substance but to a relationship. Faith is an ongoing response of trust; sin is rebellion against God. Righteousness is a right and new relationship with God. Grace is a continual gift of God. Covenant is an I-Thou relationship—"I will be your God, and you will be my people." "I have called you friends."

Trinitarian speech is about God's relatedness. There are three "persons" (subsistent relationships) in one. Further, the living God is alive in relationship. "God, if He exists," Simone Weil suggests, "is good because He delights in the existence of something other than himself."[2] The New Testament defines God as "love." We, being in the image of God, are created for relationship. We are to love our neighbor as ourselves. We are to sustain relationships with counterparts, otherwise we are "empty":

> If I speak in the tongues of men and angels….And if I have prophetic powers, and understand all mysteries and all knowledge…and have not love, I am nothing.
>
> —1 Corinthians 13:1-2 RSV

Likeness to God cannot be lived in isolation. It can only be lived in human community. We are intended to be with one another. Life is not so much "out there" or "in here" as between. Reality is known in reciprocity. "The motif is significant for me," the French artist Claude Monet stated. "What I want to reproduce is what lies between the motif and me."[3]

The biblical word that best approximates the mutuality of being is the Hebrew *shalom*. The primary meaning is "wholeness." Shalom is a condition of well-being. It is a balance among God, human beings, and all created things. All parts are interrelated. Each part participates in the whole. Thus, if one part is denied wholeness (shalom), every other part is diminished as well. The relational reality of life is grounded in the common origin in God the Creator, who continues to sustain all things.

Separate Yet Connected

Congregations are essentially relationships. First, there is the association between the "head" who is Christ and the individual parts that compose the "body." Theologian L. S. Thornton notes: "We are in Christ, not as a pebble in a box, but as a branch in a tree."[4] The other connection is between individual members with the other members. Comedian Lily Tomlin says, "We are all in this together, by ourselves."

In 1 Corinthians 12, Paul lists a number of bodily organs for the purpose of making clear that a body can function as one body only if its different parts—eye, ear, hand, foot—function differently. Separateness, differentiation, and the "self" are not denied: "Now you are the body of Christ and individually members of it" (v. 27). Within the body of Christ people are "members one of another," yet "not all the members have the same function" (Romans 12:4). "Without the members there is no body," Niebuhr mentions. "Without the body, no members."[5]

It is believed that the source of St. Paul's description of the church in 1 Corinthians 12 is a fable that had wide currency in the ancient world. The tale begins with the statement of how a republic resembles a human body. Each entity is a composite, consisting of many parts. No one of an entity's parts has the same function or performs the same services as the other parts. But if these parts of the human body were each endowed with perception and voice, this is what would be heard if a quarrel arose among them. For instance, suppose all the parts rose up against the belly. The feet would say that the whole body rests on them. The hands would contend that they handle the crafts, gather the provisions, combat the enemies, and contribute many other advantages for the common good. The shoulders would argue that they bear all the burdens; the mouth, that it speaks; the head, that it sees and hears and comprehends the other senses. Then all these parts should say to the belly, "And you, good creature, which of these things do you do?" Not to be undone by their sedition, the belly would make the defense that it sustains all, though it seems to do nothing but take in.

In relationship systems, two equal dangers exist. We can succumb to the *distancing* principle or the *dissolving* principle. The distancing threat, for example, is insisting on having one's way (1 Corinthians 13:5). The relationship is hindered. People are cut off from one another.

The dissolving threat is to fuse with another, forcing the other to be like oneself. Love guarantees that the other is truly valuable in himself or herself. The other is not an extension of me, not a possession. The other is free to be. St. Paul says that one must be "patient and kind" (v. 4), permitting the other a certain freedom. Richard John Neuhaus comments that "linkages have an insidious habit of turning into sponges."[6] There must always be a certain space between people so there can be dialogue, exchange, alongsidedness, and engagement. Being in relationship does not mean blurring distinctions. Ironically, we employ the word *committed* to signify both an attribute of steadiness leading to marriage as well as the state of being confined to a mental institution. The two questions are, What is it about love that clouds perspective? What is it about perspective that hampers love?

Reaction versus Response

Obviously a congregation has resources not available in other communities. Nonetheless the availability of the higher medicines is no guarantee that they will be used or even appreciated. We would suppose that when trouble enters a congregation, the higher medicines would be part of the treatment plan. But relationships occur within the context of emotional processes. Under certain circumstances, people react. Forces of emotionality disrupt reasoning, valuing, and decision making. Passion interferes with judgment. The "cool head" gives way to anxiety. Uncontrolled or misguided emotion bolts into reactive behaviors, some of which are startling or disgusting. The best theology—the clearest and soundest— will help little if people lack self-control and self-awareness. Under duress the thinking brain gives way to the lower, more automatic brains. Good theology as well as good sense is suspended.

Unless people respond instead of react, health will be limited. Viruses will find host cells; the immune system will be suppressed. Healing processes will be immobilized or retarded. Kathleen Norris contrasts how a Benedictine monastery and a small-town church women's group handled controversy. She illustrates the difference between reaction and response.

A monastic community in the Philippines had to confront the fact that some of the sisters participated in the public revolt against the Marcos regime. Some sisters disapproved of demonstration and the possible embarrassment of arrest. The monastic group assembled, bracketing the meeting with prayer. Each side explained their reasons:

> It was eventually decided that the nuns who were demonstrating should continue to do so; those who wished to express solidarity but were unable to march would prepare food and provide medical assistance to the demonstrators, and those who disapproved would pray for everyone. The sisters laughed and said, "If one of the conservative sisters was praying that

we young, crazy ones would come to our senses and stay off
the streets, that was O.K. We were still a community."[7]

On the other hand, Norris looks at another organization of
women in a local church. A younger member distributed a non-
partisan pamphlet containing educational materials regarding an
issue on the state ballot. Another woman started to criticize her
for bringing politics into a Bible study. Norris comments:

> This is a story of fear, a fear so pervasive that even in a small
> group of people you've known most of your life you can't
> speak up, you can't risk talking about issues. The meeting
> had begun and ended with prayer, but no one had a say, no
> one was heard, and community was diminished.[8]

Reactivity suspends, corrupts, or inhibits community—even if
prayer opens and closes a meeting.

Metanoia: Antidote to Paranoia

No group of people spends more time and energy dealing with
forgiveness than the Christian community. God's forgiveness is
a given. It cannot be reversed, modified, or altered. It is there.
Human forgiveness is slower and more spotty.

Among the favored ways of regarding the congregation, the
idea of healing and reconciliation is readily accepted. Closely
associated with reconciliation and healing in the Old and New
Testaments is "shalom"— the peace of God. Shalom can be synonymous with salvation. It means the bringing together of what
is separated, the mending of what is torn apart, the completion
of the incomplete, the overcoming of the fragments and pieces
by forgiving love.

With forgiveness, you find its companion—repentance. The
Greek word for "repentance" is *metanoia* (meaning to change
one's mind). People in their "right minds" take responsibility

for what they have done that is hurtful and offensive. They take ownership for whatever impact their sin and stupidity have had on others. They seek forgiveness for themselves. And likewise, they forgive. They are responsive to others. No person can ever be free of anything that has not been forgiven. To carry the burden of anger and grudge into the future is to allow the past to defeat us. Grace commits to the future, to a "new creation."

"Metanoia" is the antidote for "paranoia," the Greek word depicting the state of being out of one's mind. Paranoia leads to the loss of self-regulation, self-awareness, and self-definition. You cannot offer or receive forgiveness in a reactive posture. Paranoid behavior is defensive. To forgive is to release; to be forgiven is to have the future open to you.

For Reflection and Discussion

1. What "medicine" does your congregation need today to become healthier?
2. How can your congregation use the "higher medicines" to prevent disease?
3. How can the higher medicines be used in your family? In your workplace?

Chapter 8

The Immune Congregation

Organizations grow under pressure when a change or a crisis reveals new strength from all quarters.

—*Max DePree*

Leadership is always a struggle, often a feud.

—*Garry Wills*

Indeed, the values and meanings of a society become a collective immune system.

—*F. David Peat*

All the destructive organisms we know about are probably present in most people most of the time. They only take over when we get sick, when our immune defenses are not sufficient. Vision—a widely shared vision—is the immune defense system of an institution.

—*Robert Greenleaf*

The leaders deployed throughout the system are like specialized cells in the body's autoimmune system.

—*John R. O'Neil*

Self and Non-Self

Medical missionary Paul Brand set up a hypothetical choice. If for some bizarre reason doctors were forced to select for themselves (1) the immune system alone or (2) no immune system but all the resources and technology of medical science, which would they choose? Brand believes that without hesitation the physicians would choose the immune system. It is acknowledged to be the single major determinant of health and disease. The immune system is a network of cells that recognize and attack foreign invaders. The system asks one profound question: What is self, and what is not self? By distinguishing self (cells and protein native to the body) from non-self (organisms and compounds from outside the body), the immune system gets rid of any non-self entity and keeps the body's biological integrity intact.[1]

Following birth, we are protected from infection by the antibodies that originated in the body of our mother. But this immunity soon dwindles. We begin to develop our own innate resistance. Through exposure to pathogens, our body is challenged and produces an immune response. The immune system develops a "memory." So if the same pathogens appear again, the white blood cells will recognize them and rush to defend the body against them.

Wise Blood

Germs, viruses, and bacteria are always around. Whether a person is healthy or sick depends in part on his or her capacity to ward off potentially threatening microbes. In the same sense, anxious forces are ever present in the body politic. The community needs an immune response, to determine what is self and not self. The community needs to ask, for instance, if a certain action continues, whether it will enhance the mission of the congregation or detract from it. Does an individual's or a group's behavior contradict or serve the congregation's purposes? Is there clarity about who is responsible for what and accountable to whom?

The immune function, determining what does or does not benefit the congregation, is the task of leadership. Good leadership provides good immune functioning. Well before the practice of vaccination, physicians knew that people who had an infection once recovered more quickly if infected again. These people were said to have "wise blood."

Similarly, healthy congregations develop an immune system. They do not permit pathogens to inflict harm on the community. Mature leadership gives the congregation wise blood. If, hypothetically, pastors were given a choice between (1) mature, motivated leadership or (2) no such immune system but all the latest programs and techniques for running an organization, without hesitation the wise pastors would select the leadership.

Overkill

Immune systems can be our salvation and our ruin. Indeed they protect the organism from harmful microorganisms. At the same time they can betray us, as in an autoimmune reaction. Rheumatoid arthritis involves angry defense cells attacking the body's own ligaments and joints. Healthy tissues are attacked, mistaken for pathogenic invaders. Other autoimmune reactions result from keen sensitization to such things as pollen, food, animal hair, insect bites, even some medicine. For some unknown reason, the body reacts fiercely to a normally harmless substance. Someone calls it a case of "friendly fire," becoming the target of one's own defensive forces. A healthy reaction turns self-destructive. The defensive forces become the provocateur of disease.

Generally the immune system repels and rejects invading organisms without attacking the body's own tissues. But recognizing what is self and what is not self can sometimes be difficult. Chemically, foreign products are only slightly different from a body's own molecules. Sometimes, instead of simply tolerating an alien substance, the immune system erupts into overkill. Even though the foreign matter is innocuous, the immune system reads it as a troublemaker. An immunologist refers to the autoimmune reaction as the "dyslexia of the immune system."

The system misreads what is actually there. The body destroys not only the invading cells but also its own tissue.

There are parallels between how our physical bodies function and how our relationship systems function. We relate to one another in the ways biological cells respond to one another. Autoimmunity in relationship systems means the leaders who function as the immune system overreact. The immune system of common sense is suppressed. Normally reasonable people exaggerate their defense of the system. They violate their own good judgment. Someone, for example, raises a troubling but necessary question at a congregational meeting. An air of tension grows. An awkwardness develops in the group. The pastor suddenly throws shame to the winds and berates the questioner:

"If you were a more active member…"
"Why ask such a question of hard working people?"
"When did you become an authority on theology?"

Powerfully designed for self-preservation, immune capacities employ excessive force. Like the pastor above, anyone can be in more danger from their own mindless, defensive behaviors (autoimmune reaction) than from those who offend them. The enemy is us.

Immunity Equals Integrity

The immunological forces of the body ensure both survival and integrity. They protect the organism against destructive pathogens. Immunity is effectively designed to keep things apart. No immunology, no survival. The immune system provides integrity as well. Just as immune capacities separate what belongs to the body from what is foreign to it, likewise we must have immune capacities in a community to distinguish what is "ours" and what is "other's." Without this capacity, a community will not know what behaviors are beneficial or harmful, what actions add to or detract from the stewardship of the whole, and what responses are faith-driven or expedient measures. Immunity preserves the community.

In the following story, you will recognize effective immune functioning. Mature leaders serve as the congregation's immune system in the face of potential disease. They bring clarity and objectivity to a tense situation. Of course, clarity is not always comforting to some.

Evergreen Hills Church will soon celebrate its twentieth anniversary. It has approximately 550 members, about the same level as five years ago. Pastor Jim Roth has been there for seven years. He is the second pastor, having succeeded the founding minister, Porter Roberts.

Generally, the pastor and the people have fared well. There is some disappointment that growth has reached a plateau, but Pastor Roth has provided excellent pastoral care and has initiated several successful new programs. Actually the area around the church's location has built up. The congregation has little space for expansion. What growth is happening is seven to eight miles to the north in Cascade.

What is known by several lay leaders but not the vast majority is that Jim and his wife, Melanie, will be divorcing soon. All but one of the nine leaders want Jim to remain as the congregation's pastor. The judicatory supervisor has said that he will support the lay leaders in whatever action they believe is best.

The divorce is a mutual decision. There is little rancor, but both Jim and Melanie are depressed about the dissolution of their marriage. Melanie plans to leave town as soon as she finds a new job. She will take their five-year-old daughter with her.

What Jim has not fully revealed to his lay leaders is his intent to explore a relationship with a woman in the community, not a member of Evergreen Hills. Jim met Brittany at a municipal gathering. They both serve on the Mayor's Task Force on Youth, which explores ways to curb teenage vandalism, random acts of teenage violence, and teenage pregnancy. Brittany is divorced with two daughters, thirteen and fifteen years old. Jim has every intention to be discrete about the relationship. He feels, however, that the two of them are only beginning to explore the emotional aspects of their relationship. He chooses to say nothing to anyone.

For several weeks, a strange atmosphere hovers over the congregation. Melanie has left without explanation, and speculation circulates about what is happening. When the congregation is notified of the divorce, Melanie's departure, and Jim's desire to stay as the pastor, only a few sporadic rumblings occur. Nonetheless, rumors and hearsay make the rounds. Two people decide to leave the congregation.

Jim and Brittany started to see each other approximately three months after Jim and Melanie's divorce was finalized. Realizing that the relationship could potentially be "serious," Jim was prepared to tell the church leaders. Before he had a chance to do it himself, one of the nine leaders stormed into Jim's office, raging at Jim for not sharing information about Brittany. Todd, a forty-one-year-old father of three girls, was the only leader who originally thought that Jim should resign because of his divorce. Jim calmly recited all the events of the relationship and his intention to notify the board members. Unmoved, Todd vowed to force Jim's removal. "There are lots of others," he warned Jim, "who think the way I do."

Later that day Kristen arrived at Jim's office. Todd's wife had called her, relaying the news of Jim's and Brittany's relationship. As chair of the board, Kristen wanted to hear Jim's story. Although she thought Jim did not use good judgment in not notifying the board, she trusted Jim.

That evening Kristen's husband, Dick, called Jim at home to offer his support. But Jim also received a telephone call from Todd's brother Scott, who resorted to shaming Jim: "You are the spiritual leader. You must be above reproach. Why didn't you leave when you got divorced? Why did you put Todd in this embarrassing position?"

At the next meeting of the board, Jim presented the background and the development of his relationship with Brittany. He assured them that the relationship was "discrete and moral." Brittany, he attested, was an honorable person. But Todd insisted that Jim resign immediately. And he threatened that if Jim did not resign, he would reveal "the real story" about Jim and Brittany.

Kristen, Tara, Mitsy, and Fred disagreed. They challenged Todd. If he had information ("the real story"), he should talk to Jim directly. The other board members were silent, appearing neutral. Later two of the silent four would vote in favor of Jim remaining as pastor at Evergreen Hills.

Todd refused to speak with Jim. When people asked him what else he knew, Todd simply retorted, "Well, what do you think happened?" After six months Todd, along with a group of seven other people, left Evergreen Hills.

As with most stories, this one included many nuances, details, and surprises. For our purposes—examining the leaders' functioning as an immune system—let us look at three items: Todd's autoimmune reaction, the efforts of the majority on the board to search for clarity, and the immune response, that is, making a decision about what would happen.

The Healthy Response

Todd's reactive behavior resembles the autoimmune reaction. He exhibits poor self-control in this particular circumstance. His deep anxiety inhibits his thinking capacities. Todd's threats and vague claim that he possessed information indicate he was operating in a survival, self-preserving mode. Allowed to continue, Todd could have done damage to the "living tissue" of the congregation.

Still, Todd's reactivity is *not the problem*. Anxiety is always present in community, even as viruses are in the physical body. Because Todd could not find host cells to amplify his anxiousness, infection could not take hold. The majority functioned effectively as an immune system. They pursued clarity; they made a decision. The leaders focused on their own thinking capacities, not on the functioning of Todd.

In a congregation, reactivity may take the form of compliance or rebellion, attack or withdrawal, tantrums or apathy. The type of virus is essentially unimportant. What counts is the immune response—clear convictions leading to thought-out positions, specific goals guiding decisions. *If leaders are as anxious and reactive as the people they serve, those served will not be served well.*

The Watermelon Hunter

Systems thinking provides a useful concept: self-differentiation. It shares with the immune system a basic function: to define what is self or not self, to differentiate what is native, what is foreign.

Self-differentiation in emotional processes refers to the amount of self available to an individual, such as an individual's overall maturity, level of functioning, and the degree of responsibility for self. It is the capacity to choose a course of direction and to stay the course when reactive people want to reroute you. It is the ability to stay focused on your own functioning while being aware of others. Self-differentiation is the ability to stand up and be counted in matters of principle and belief and yet remain with family and community. It is the ability in anxious circumstances to regulate one's own reactivity by thinking. Differentiation is to take a position in the midst of emotional forces and still remain in touch with others.

In an emotional system, the leader's self-differentiating capacities greatly influence the entire organization. An ancient Sufi tale illustrates how differentiation affects community life:

> Once upon a time, there was a man who strayed from his own country into the world known as the Land of Fools. He soon saw a number of people fleeing in terror from a field where they had been trying to reap wheat. "There is a monster in that field," they told him. He looked, and saw that it was a watermelon.

He offered to kill the "monster" for them. When he had cut the melon from its stalk, he took a slice and began to eat it. The people became even more terrified of him than they had been of the melon. They drove him away with pitchforks, crying, "He will kill us next, unless we get rid of him."

It so happened that at another time another man also strayed into the Land of Fools, and the same thing started to happen to him. But, instead of offering to help them with the "monster," he agreed with them that it must be dangerous, and by tiptoeing away from it with them he gained their confidence. He spent a long time with them in their houses until he could teach them, little by little, the basic facts which would enable them not only to lose their fear of melons, but even to cultivate them themselves.[2]

The Land of the Fools is the territory of anxious reactivity. The first "leader" fails to affect the emotional field in a positive manner. The leader neither defines self nor stays in touch. Rather, he takes responsibility for others. He tries to "fix" them. The second leader works on staying in touch. He teaches and affects the thinking brain. Further, he does not "feed" the people's anxiety. They become imaginative, growing their own watermelons.

Functional Range

What, then, should we look for in the functioning of a leader? The following lists summarize the range between undifferentiation and differentiation.

Undifferentiation

Opts for Certainty: Uses black/white thinking (psychologist Alfred Adler refers to either/or thinking as a form of arrested development, the way children think); wants quick fix; pushes for resolution to ease own discomfort with emotional pain, ambiguity, or cognitive dissonance.

Avoids Self: Resists insight; lacks awareness of self; behaves more reactively and mindlessly; has fewer responses available to handle life.

Looks Outside of Self: Takes little responsibility for self and blames others; sees only what is exterior (anxiety forces one to observe threat, condition, what is outside of self); has little sense of connectedness and the mutual influence of behavior.

Forces Others to Adapt: Functions willfully (one way or no way); pushes and pulls on almost anything; wants others to change; coerces or manipulates.

Seeks Cessation of Pain: Shifts own anxiety to others; blames, accuses, and whines; seeks to eliminate person/event that activates one's own anxiety.

Differentiation

Takes a Stand: Works on self-definition; functions on basis of values, principles, and beliefs; knows what one believes, stays the course, and commits to the process.

Focuses on Self: Increases self-awareness; looks at own "stuckness"; modifies own exaggeration of instinctual forces (anxiety); attends to own behavior; makes changes in self.

Stays Connected to Others: Sees life organically ("members of one another"); tolerates differences; encourages dialogue.

Sets Clear Goals: Defines self from within, not over against others; knows where one is going; maintains larger view; lives with a purpose in mind; seeks clarity.

Accepts Challenge: Moves forward; stretches; knows that "pain" arises when one leads; stays focused on conviction and direction.

Ruin or Salvation

Earlier, I stated that the immune system can be our ruin or salvation. Obviously leadership can be the same for a congregation. Leadership, like the immune system, can make two kinds of mistakes—failing to resist when it should and attacking something when it should not. The first type of error results from poor response, so that a disease (reactivity) that should have been dealt with sooner becomes critical. The second kind of mistake is a consequence of mounting too much force in response to minute chemical differences, attacking even the body's cells.

Leaders can be the "salvation" of a congregation. Well differentiated, they respond with a wide repertoire of responses. They give the congregation "wise blood," wisdom derived from countless challenges to the church's integrity. Leaders can be the "ruin" too—if they do not resist alien forces, if they overreact. Knowing a leader's level of differentiation, no one can predict exact behaviors. But we can generalize that differentiated people will accept a situation as a challenge, behave with greater flexibility, and consider different options. They will be less driven by automatic processes, which alone allows for a wider range of behavior and a more creative response.

For Reflection and Discussion

1. Suppose you were a leader at Evergreen Hills Church (pages 98–101). What immunity would you want to bring to the situation? How would you go about making that happen?
2. If "good leadership provides good immune functioning," what are you and the other leaders of your congregation doing to build immunity (pages 103–105)?
3. Review the case studies in chapter 4 (pages 48–56). What might the leaders of each congregation do to develop the congregation's immunity?

Chapter 9

An Ounce of Prevention Is
Worth a Pound of Intervention

*Life can be understood backwards: but it must be lived
forward.*
                                        —*Søren Kierkegaard*

*The vision is a picture of what the organization will look like
when the organization has achieved its mission.*
                                        —*Peter Stroh*

*The healthy society, like the healthy body, is not the one
that has taken the most medicine. It is the one in which the
internal health building force is in the best shape.*
                                        —*Peter Senge*

*What God does first and best and most is to trust His people
with this moment in history. He trusts them to do what must
be done for the sake of the whole community.*
                                        —*Walter Brueggemann*

A Grand Old Church

Main Street Church has survived innumerable changes to its
surrounding environment. It is situated in a district called "the
Gardens" because of the trees and flowers along its boulevard
and in its small parks. Ivy and other crawling vines adorn many
of the buildings in the district.

In 1916 Main Street opened its door. Its original white
frame building gave way to a concrete structure in 1926. For

the next two decades, Main Street enjoyed the reputation of being a "progressive" congregation. Three successive pastors with oratorical skills gave Main Street a strong pulpit.

After World War II, the ethnic composition of the congregation slowly changed. The names now appearing on mailboxes reflected the transition—from Porter to Perez, Roberts to Romano, Williams to Wu. By 1960, Main Street's ethnic transformation seemed almost complete. The Baileys and the Scotts were the mere holdovers from the past. Tempted to leave for greener pastures (the swelling suburbs), Main Street voted to stay in the city. In 1979 the congregation again considered a possible relocation. Fire had destroyed half of the building. The question: Should we spend "that much" money to repair the facility when dwindling in numbers? The congregation chose to stay in the Gardens. For the next ten years, four different pastors served Main Street. In 1989 Pastor Heidi arrived. Combining savvy with compassion, she prepared the congregation for the future.

A Breath of Fresh Air

To prevent disease and to promote health, people can implement an infinite variety of responses. Heidi's action is offered as an example, not a universal formula. It is an illustration, not a prescription. She responded to a special set of circumstances; she made certain choices because she was pastor of Main Street congregation in the Gardens district of a city.

Heidi will tell you that she works diligently on her capacity to self-differentiate. "If we are too connected, we won't challenge each other and create differences," she explained to a lay leader. "If we are too oppositional, we won't be connected enough and see likenesses." Heidi is able to take "I positions" with members and yet stay in touch with them. In a stroke of genius, Heidi once told the congregation: "I care about you. I won't always know when you need me. I need you to let me know when you need me." Not only did Heidi affirm her care for the people, but also she encouraged her members to be responsible for themselves when they need to be cared for and to ask.

Upon her arrival at Main Street, Heidi found a cautious people, caught in old habits and depressed in spirit. In her mind she had decided, "I will not rescue or save these people. They are needy; they are looking for Mother Teresa. I'm Heidi." In one of her most recent sermons, Heidi referred to Toni Morrison's Nobel lecture before the Swedish Academy. The lecture took the form of a meditation on a folk tale.

> An old, blind woman lives on the town's outskirts. Several children decide to fool her. One of them says he has a bird in his hand and asks her to tell him if it is alive or dead. The woman is silent for a long time. Finally she announces, "I don't know whether the bird you are holding is dead or alive, but what I do know is that it is in your hands. It is in your hands."

Heidi says the bird is a metaphor for stewardship. "The question is not whether our congregation is dead or alive," Heidi concludes. "The question is whether or not it's in responsible and responsive hands."

The Right Focus

Intuitively, Heidi knows how easy it would be for the people to focus on their weaknesses, their problems, and their congregation as a shadow of what was once a beaming light. To keep the congregation focused on its strengths, resources, and future options, she realizes, is to keep the congregation on the road to health.

Heidi attended a pastors' conference on leadership. She did a lot of reflection on the speaker's story about the flying Wallendas, the world's greatest family of tightrope walkers and aerialists. Karl Wallenda once mentioned that except for walk-ing the tightrope, everything else in life was waiting. He had a passion, an internal capacity for concentration on the task. Karl Wallenda slipped and fell to his death between two high-rise buildings in San Juan, Puerto Rico. Wallenda fell clutching the balancing pole. Following his own advice to family members, he held on to the pole. Never, he had warned, drop the pole, lest it hurt someone below. He performed the aerial act without a safety net below. Later, his wife reported that there had been a sudden shift in Karl's approach to his work. For the first time, she said, her husband had been focusing on falling, instead of on walking the tightrope. Never before had he personally supervised the attachment of the guide wires. That time he did.

At the annual leadership retreat, Heidi led a spirited dis-cussion of the Wallenda story. "Where's our focus?" she asked. "Are we concentrating on falling?" Trudy, who worked for the city's department of human services, mentioned that struggling families have scant awareness of their strengths. Not recogniz-ing their strengths is one reason they stay in a cycle of extreme struggle.

Persistent Pursuit

An ounce of prevention may well be worth more than a pound of intervention, but prevention may be neglected or scorned nonetheless. Systems favor stability. People become loyal to their own suffering. Oddly, they may refuse to change even if things might improve. Though matters are quite different now, Heidi remembers the early years at Main Street. She recalls saying that to change anything at Main Street was like playing tennis under eight feet of water. She came to Main Street with several goals in mind. She used her stamina to pursue them. "One of the best things I did," she mentioned "was to persevere. I had to stretch faith into hope." (Incidentally, patients who are "fighters" have better quality of life and survival rates than passive patients.)

A century and a half ago, Viennese physician Ignaz Semmelweiss noted that women in a clinic staffed by medical personnel
were three times as likely to contract childbed fever as those in a
clinic staffed by midwives. Childbed fever was the result of strep-
tococci infecting the uterus. Semmelweiss discovered that doctors
went directly from doing autopsies on women who fell prey to
childbed fever to performing pelvic examinations on women in
labor. He suggested that the doctors served as the transmitters of
the infectious agent. The doctors who washed their hands in a
disinfectant had far fewer infections among their patients.

Dismissed from his post for purporting that doctors were
causing the deaths of patients, Semmelweiss desperately sought
to save thousands of women who were dying unnecessarily. He
was ignored; he was dispatched to an insane asylum. At age
forty-seven, Semmelweiss died.[1]

Preventive efforts can be thwarted. People will not automatically do what is healthiest for them. Yet we know hope is an en-
hancer of bodily health, and losing hope can have a deadly effect.
In *The Recovery of Confidence*, Professor John Gardner urges us
to be more hopeful. It is hope that pours people back into life.
Hope, he believes, does not assume a cure has been found for
all of life's ills or that unfavorable odds are unreal. "There is the
resilience of the human spirit," he writes, "We were designed
for struggle."[2] Hope pushes us to persevere. As a rule the body
flourishes with activity and exercise. Would not the same hold
true for the human spirit? It needs challenge. The spirit needs
activity and exercise. It needs stretching. Indeed, Heidi's spiritually stubborn side is what eventually disarmed the demons of
resistance.

A significant measure of the health of the congregation is
not where it stands in moments of comfort and ease, but rather,
where it stands at times of challenge and crisis. In healthy congregations, leaders focus on their *response* to conditions, not the
conditions alone. They are guided more by their own horizons
than by the things they see on the horizon.

Psychiatrist Joel Dimsdale studied survivors of the Nazi death camps. What kept them going? He says the human quality that kept these prisoners alive was "blind, naked hope." Further, essayist Norman Cousins, surveying over six hundred oncologists, asked what factors in their patients they judged important. Over 90 percent replied that the supreme attitude was *hope*.[3]

Looking Ahead

Having once lived in Oakland, Trudy knew Gertrude Stein's famous statement about the California city: "There's no there there." With a big smile, Trudy said that Stein was actually referring to Main Street before Heidi came: "There's no there there." Trudy added, "Heidi gave us a vision. A vision doesn't change 'there,' but it surely changed our response to 'there.'"

Vision offers meaning; vision instills hope; vision directs energy. Edward Hays tells a story that comes from the early Christian hermits of Egypt:

> It seems that a young aspirant to holiness once came to visit the hermitage of an old holy man who was sitting in the doorway of his quarters at sunset. The old man's dog stretched out across the threshold as the young spiritual seeker presented his problem to the holy man. "Why is it, Abba, that some who seek God come to the desert and are zealous in prayer but leave after a year or so, while others, like you, remain faithful to the quest for a lifetime?"
>
> The old man smiled and replied, "Let me tell you a story:
>
> "One day I was sitting here quietly in the sun with my dog. Suddenly a large white rabbit ran across in front of us. Well, my dog jumped up, barking loudly, and took off after that big rabbit. He chased the rabbit over the hills with a passion. Soon, other dogs joined him, attracted by his barking. What a sight it was, as the pack of dogs ran barking across

the creeks, up stony embankments and through thickets and thorns! Gradually, however, one by one, the other dogs dropped out of the pursuit, discouraged by the course and frustrated by the chase. Only my dog continued to hotly pursue the white rabbit.

"In that story, young man, is the answer to your question."

The young man sat in confused silence. Finally, he said, "Abba. I don't understand. What is the connection between the rabbit chase and the quest for holiness?"

"You fail to understand," answered the old hermit, "because you failed to ask the obvious question. Why didn't the other dogs continue the chase? And the answer to that question is that they had not *seen* the rabbit. Unless you see your prey, the chase is just too difficult. You will lack the passion and determination necessary to perform all the hard work required by the discipline of your spiritual exercises."[4]

If the way forward is unclear, it is difficult to be wholehearted. How can you tell whether you are "stuck" unless you have a direction? If the vision is vague, people lose interest.

When to Weave a Parachute

When Heidi arrived in 1989, she immediately proposed a 75th anniversary celebration in 1991, only eighteen months away. Slowly enthusiasm grew. A letter was sent out to former members, asking for donations to defray some of the costs and for stories and memorabilia. The daughter of one of the former pastors agreed to pay for the writing of the church history. Other monies were received for needed repairs. As time drew closer to the event, excitement ran high. A variety of events and services would happen over a three-month period. Edna Mae, Trudy's sister, recommended a special $20,000 thank offering, earmarked for a children's center at Main Street. Offerings and gifts would be solicited from former members as well as current ones. The children's center would provide day care, after-school care, tutorial services for grade school children, and seed money for an all-volunteer health clinic. The congregation received $27,000, including a $10,000 donation from local merchants.

In retrospect many members cite the 75th anniversary event as the pivotal shift in Main Street's spirit and direction. They thought less and less about "falling." The downside of the good that was happening involved Roberto Sanchez and Bill Sauls. They believed Heidi had accrued too much power. They charged her with using Main Street as a stepping stone to "something bigger." They complained about her privately but never publicly. Leadership, she knew, elicits reactivity. Still, she felt perturbed that neither of the men would confront her directly.

Roberto had lost some of his power. He felt hurt. Often the wounded turn their anxiety into reactivity. But Roberto had to be careful because his sister Rosa strongly supported Heidi. Bill Sauls was another story. Bill joined anything that was negative. He had little capacity to rejoice. Bill Sauls could be compared to the man who put his nose in limburger cheese and came up saying the whole world stinks. Many people accepted Bill Sauls in spite of his maddening behavior.

Working with the leaders, Heidi pushed for a policy on criticism. They worked out a procedure that was fair. The congregation approved it overwhelmingly. Of course, this action itself did not inhibit secrets, rumors, or misinformation from circulating. The "viruses," though, never found host cells to be carriers. The system was not infected.

The anniversary celebration, the special thank offering, the policy on criticism were all preventive measures. They keep the sky from falling down. Indeed, the time to weave a parachute is not just before one must jump. The parachute is woven *ahead* of time.

The Holy Imagination

"The inventive, creative potential of the human brain," Edgar Jackson remarks, "is the most significant product of creation."[5] But if we are anxious, we are less imaginative. The neo-cortex is underemployed. Consequently our learning abilities diminish as well. A recent study indicated that children who are unimaginative are more likely to act violently than imaginative children. The unimaginative cannot imagine alternatives. If sensory information is uncomfortable or threatening, they lash out in typical R-system defensiveness. The imaginative child, however, can imagine alternative ways to handle the situation. Imagination offers resiliency, flexibility.

Congregations function in similar ways. The unimaginative ones are more violent (nasty, willful, deceptive) when they are threatened. More imaginative congregations draw up a list of options.

Remember the story of the three clergy on a mountain top, escaping a monstrous flood. The waters are rising steadily. One cleric says they need a miracle to survive. A second one calls for immediate salvation. The third, however, says that he thinks they will have to learn how to live under water. Heidi's creative role at Main Street was about "learning how to live under water"—no demands for miracles, cures, painlessness. "When I was a youngster in Minnesota," Heidi said, "I remember the pastor saying to the farmers: 'When you pray for potatoes, bring a hoe in hand.'" Heidi had no doubt about what God had graciously provided Main Street. But she also knew something about "the whole" or "the system" or "the organic." God's provisions often came through people's responses.

Trudy hastily called a congregational meeting on a Friday night. Perhaps eighty to ninety attended. "Massive, inoperable," Trudy announced, "six months to live if she's lucky." Heidi had cancer.

"I want you to go home tonight and pray for our sister, our pastor, her family, this congregation. And tomorrow morning it's still on as planned. We are going to work on our little garden. Bring a hoe."

For Reflection and Discussion

1. What are you and your congregation doing to prevent disease and promote health?
2. Review the genogram you developed when you reflected on chapter 3. What has inhibited the congregation's health? What has promoted health? Why have these factors been important? What changes would make your congregation healthier?
3. How can you and the other leaders of your congregation enhance your congregation's health?

Notes

Preface 1996

1. Kenneth R. Pelletier, *Sound Mind, Sound Body: A New Model for Lifelong Health* (New York: Simon and Schuster, 1994), 164.

2. Larry Dossey, *Meaning and Medicine* (New York: Bantam Books, 1991), 212.

3. Kathleen Norris, *Dakota: A Spiritual Geography* (Boston: Houghton Mifflin Company, 1993), 160-170.

Chapter 1, Life Is All of a Piece

1. Edgar Jackson, *Understanding Health* (Philadelphia: Trinity Press International, 1989), 86.

2. Lewis Thomas, *The Youngest Science* (Toronto: Bantam Books, 1984). 200.

3. Charles M. Johnston, *Necessary Wisdom* (Berkeley, Calif: ICD Press, 1991), 207.

4. A review of foreign words reveals the long association between health and wholeness. The Old English word *hal* is the source of the word "whole," and *haelen* is the source of "healing." The Latin word *sanus* (from which sanity is derived) means "fitness," and the Greek word *hygeia* indicates "soundness." The Greek *systema* signifies "whole." The German word *heil* carries the double connotation of "health" and "salvation."

5. Pelletier, *Sound Mind, Sound Body: A New Model for Lifelong Health* (New York: Simon and Schuster, 1994), 133.

6. Blair Justice, *Who Gets Sick* (Los Angeles: Jeremy P. Tarcher, Inc., 1987), 142.

Chapter 2, Ten Principles of Health

1. The ten principles are adapted from Edgar Jackson, *Understanding Health* (Philadelphia: Trinity Press International, 1989), 62-74; and Andrew Weil, *Health and Healing* (Boston, Houghton Mifflin Company, 1988), 52-62.

2. Hans Selye, *Stress without Distress* (New York: New American Library, 1974), 22-23.

3. Max DePree, *Leadership Jazz* (New York: Dell Publishing, 1992), 46.

4. The Institute of Noetic Sciences with William Pool, *The Heart of Healing* (Atlanta: Turner Publishing, Inc., 1993), 60.

5. James J. Lynch, *The Broken Heart* (New York: Basic Books, Inc., 1977). 3.

6. Wendell Berry, *Another Turn of the Crank* (Washington, D.C.: Counterpoint. 1995), 90.

7. Selye. *Stress without Distress,* 6, 7.

8. Robert Ornstein, *The Healing Brain* (New York: Simon and Schuster, 1987), 12.

Chapter 3, Promoting Healthy Congregations

1. Susan Sontag, *Illness as Metaphor* (New York: Vintage Books, 1977), 1.

2. Leland R. Kaiser, *Managing at the Ninth Level* (Brighton, Cob.: Brighton Books. 1990), 3.

3. Aaron Antonovsky, *Unraveling the Mystery of Health* (San Francisco: Jossey-Barr Publications, 1988). XI-XII.

4. Robert Greenleaf, *Servant Leadership* (New York: Paulist Press, 1977). 13.

5. Marc Ian Barasch, *The Healing Path* (New York: G.P. Putnam's Sons, 1995), 309.

6. Paul Brand and Philip Yancy, *Pain: The Gift Nobody Wants* (New York: HarperCollins, 1993), 244, 270.

Notes

119

Chapter 4, Congregations at Risk

1. Charles Hampden-Turner. *Maps of the Mind: Charts and Concepts of the Mind and Its Labyrinths* (New York: Macmillan Publishing Co., Inc., 1981), 9-10.

2. Margaret J. Wheatley, *Leadership and the New Science* (San Francisco: Berrett-Koehler Publishers, 1992), 16.

3. Paul Brand and Philip Yancy, *Pain: The Gift Nobody Wants* (New York: HarperCollins, 1993), 188.

4. Randolph M. Nesse and George C. Williams, *Why We Get Sick* (New York: Times Books, 1994), 35.

Chapter 5, Infectious Anxiety

1. Dietrich Bonhoeffer, *Life Together* (San Francisco: HarperCollins, 1954), 89.

2. M. Scott Peck, *The People of the Lie* (New York: Simon and Schuster, 1983), 74.

3. David W. Augsburger, *Conflict Mediation across Cultures* (Louisville, Ky.: Westminster John Knox, 1992), 154.

4. Bonhoeffer, *Life Together*, 89.

5. Richard Restak, *The Brain Has a Mind of Its Own* (New York: Crown Trade Paperbacks, 1991), 13.

6. Ibid. 51-57. For additional information on the brain, see Restak, *The Brain Has a Mind of Its Own*, and Daniel Coleman, *Emotional Intelligence* (New York: Bantam Books, 1995).

Chapter 6, The Coconut Captivity of the Church

1. Robert Pirsig, *Zen and the Art of Motorcycle Maintenance* (New York: William Morrow & Co., 1974), 312.

2. Larry Dossey, *Meaning and Medicine* (New York: Bantam Books, 1991), 128-129.

3. Kenneth R. Pelletier, *Sound Mind, Sound Body: A New Model for Lifelong Health,* 18-19.

4. Alvin Toffler, *Future Shock* (New York: Bantam Books,1970), 9.

5. Daniel Goleman, *Emotional Intelligence* (New York: Bantam Books, 1995). 38.

6. Maggie Scarf, *Intimate Worlds: Life Inside the Family* (New York: Random House, 1995), 225

7. H. Richard Niebuhr, *The Purpose of the Church and Its Ministry* (New York: Harper and Row Publishers, 1979), 83.

8. See Senge, *The Fifth Discipline* (New York: Dell Currency, 1990).

Chapter 7, The Higher Medicines

1. Martin Luther. *Church Postil Sermons,* vol. 1, 10-11.

2. Sallie McFague, *The Body of God* (Minneapolis, Minn.: Fortress Press, 1993), 51.

3. Paul R. Sponheim, *Faith and the Other* (Minneapolis, Minn.: Fortress Press, 1993), 194.

4. John A. T. Robinson, *The Body: A Study in Pauline Theology* (Chicago: Henry Regnery Co, 1932), p. 62.

5. H. Richard Niebuhr, *The Purpose of the Church and its Ministry* (New York: Harper and Row, 1956), 42.

6. Richard John Neuhaus, *Freedom for Ministry* (New York: Harper and Row Publishers, 1979), 129.

7. Kathleen Norris, *Dakota: A Spiritual Geography* (Boston: Houghton Mifflin Company, 1993), 114.

8. Ibid.

Chapter 8, The Immune Congregation

1. Paul Brand and Philip Yancy, *Pain: The Gift Nobody Wants* (New York: HarperCollins, 1993), 240.

2. Idries Shah, *The Way of the Sufi* (New York: E.P. Dutton and Company, Inc., 1975), 207.

Chapter 9, An Ounce of Prevention Is Worth a Pound of Intervention

1. Edgar Jackson, *Understanding Health* (Philadelphia: Trinity Press International, 1989), 58-59.

2. Pelletier, *Sound Mind, Sound Body: A New Model for Lifelong Health,* 197.

3. Blair Justice. *Who Gets Sick* (Los Angeles, Jeremy P. Tarcher, Inc., 1987), 70.

4. Edward Hays, *In Pursuit of the Great White Rabbit: Reflections on a Practical Spirituality* (Easton, Kan.: Forest of Peace Books), 10-11.

5. Jackson, *Understanding Health,* 31.

Bibliography

Antonovsky, Aaron. *Unraveling the Mystery of Health*. San Francisco: Jossey-Barr Publishers, 1988.

Augsburger, David W. *Conflict Mediation across Cultures*. Louisville, Ky.: Westminster John Knox, 1992.

Barasch, Marc Ian. *The Healing Path*. New York: G. P. Putnam's Sons, 1995.

Berry, Wendell. *Another Turn of the Crank*. Washington, D.C.: Counterpoint, 1995.

Bonhoeffer, Dietrich. *Life Together*. San Francisco: Harper Collins, 1954.

Brand, Paul. *The Forever Feast*. Ann Arbor, Mich.: Servant Publication, 1993.

Brand, Paul, and Philip Yancy. *Pain: The Gift Nobody Wants*. New York: HarperCollins, 1993.

Davis, Joel. *Defending the Body*. New York: Atheneum, 1989.

DePree, Max. *Leadership Jazz*. New York: Dell Publishing, 1992.

Dossey, Larry. *Meaning and Medicine*. New York: Bantam Books, 1991.

Fettner, Ann Giudici. *The Science of Viruses*. New York: William Morrow, 1990.

Goleman, Daniel. *Emotional Intelligence*. New York: Bantam Books, 1995.

Greenleaf, Robert K. *Servant Leadership*. New York: Paulist Press, 1977.

Hampden-Turner, Charles. *Maps of the Mind: Charts and Concepts of the Mind and Its Labyrinths*. New York: Macmillan Publishing Co., Inc., 1981.

Hays, Edward. *In Pursuit of the Great White Rabbit: Reflections on a Practical Spirituality*. Easton, Ks.: Forest of Peace Books, 1990.

Heifetz, Ronald A. *Leadership without Easy Answers.* Cambridge, Mass.: The Belknap Press of Harvard University Press, 1994.

The Institute of Noetic Sciences with William Pool. *The Heart of Healing.* Atlanta: Turner Publishing, Inc., 1993.

Jackson, Edgar. *Understanding Health.* Philadelphia: Trinity Press International, 1989.

Johnston, Charles M. *Necessary Wisdom.* Berkeley. Calif., ICD Press, 1991.

Justice, Blair. *Who Gets Sick.* Los Angeles: Jeremy P. Tarcher, Inc., 1987.

Kaiser, Leland R. *Managing at the Ninth Level.* Brighton, Cob.: Brighton Books, 1990.

Kerr, Michael, and Murray Bowen. *Family Evaluation.* New York: W.W. Norton and Company, 1988.

Locke, Steven, and Douglas Colligen. *The Healer Within.* New York: New American Library, 1986.

Lynch, James J. *The Broken Heart.* New York: Basic Books, Inc., Publishers, 1977.

Marty, Martin E. *Health and Medicine in the Lutheran Tradition.* New York: Crossroad, 1983.

McFague, Sallie. *The Body of God.* Minneapolis, Minn: Fortress Press, 1993.

McGoldrick, Monica. *You Can Go Home Again.* New York: W.W. Norton and Company, 1995.

Nesse, Randolph M., and George C. Williams. *Why We Get Sick.* New York: Times Books, 1994.

Neuhaus, Richard John. *Freedom for Ministry.* New York: Harper and Row Publishers, 1979.

Niebuhr, H. Richard. *The Purpose of the Church and Its Ministry.* New York: Harper and Row, 1956.

Norris, Kathleen. *Dakota: A Spiritual Geography.* Boston: Houghton Muffin Company. 1993.

Oden, Thomas C. *Crisis Ministries.* New York: Crossroad, 1986.

Ornstein, Robert. *The Healing Brain.* New York: Simon and Schuster, 1987.

Palmer, Parker J. *The Company of Strangers.* New York: Crossroad, 1981.

Peat, F. David. *The Philosopher's Stone.* New York: Bantam Books, 1991.

Peck, M. Scott. *The People of the Lie.* New York: Simon and Schuster, 1983.

Pelletier, Kenneth R. *Sound Mind, Sound Body: A New Model for Lifelong Health.* New York: Simon and Schuster. 1994.

Restak, Richard. *The Brain Has a Mind of Its Own.* New York: Crown Trade Paperbacks, 1991.

Selye, Hans. *Stress without Distress.* New York: New American Library, 1974.

Senge, Peter. *The Fifth Discipline.* New York: Doubleday Currency, 1990.

Shah, Idries. *The Way of the Sufi.* New York: E. P. Dutton and Company, Inc., 1975.

Sponheim, Paul R. *Faith and the Other.* Minneapolis, Minn.: Fortress Press, 1993.

Thomas, Lewis. *The Fragile Species.* New York: MacMillan Publishing Company, 1992.

———. *The Lives of a Cell.* New York: The Viking Press, 1974.

———. *The Youngest Science.* Toronto: Bantam Books, 1984.

Well, Andrew. *Health and Healing.* Boston: Houghton Mifflin Company, 1988.

———. *Spontaneous Healing.* New York: Alfred A. Knopf, 1995.

Wheatley, Margaret J. *Leadership and the New Science.* San Francisco: Berett-Koehler Publishers, 1992.